Prayers for Living

500 Prayers for Public and Private Worship

— ROSALIND BROWN —

Sacristy
Press

Sacristy Press
PO Box 612, Durham, DH1 9HT

www.sacristy.co.uk

First published in 2021 by Sacristy Press, Durham

Sacristy Limited, registered in England & Wales, number 7565667

British Library Cataloguing-in-Publication Data
A catalogue record for the book is available from the British Library

Paperback ISBN 978-1-78959-188-0
Hardback ISBN 978-1-78959-197-2

Contents

Preface: Prayers for private and public worship v

The needs of the world.. 1

General world needs 2

People with power or influence in the world 5

Justice and wellbeing for all 11

War and peace... 14

Refugees and people in danger................................. 18

Disasters... 26

Rescue, emergency and aid workers 29

National and local life 31

Government and public life 32

National and local services 34

Local community life.. 48

Daily Life... 53

Living faithfully 54

Morning, noon and evening.................................... 73

Homes and hospitality... 80

Work... 81

Education and learning.. 85

Creativity and the arts 88

Families and friends 91

Relationships... 92

People and families under stress or with special needs........... 96

Children.. 100

Older people 103

People in Need **107**

People in need. 108

People in poverty 119

People who are overwhelmed, in despair or grieving 121

Sickness and suffering 130

People who respond to need. 137

Creation. **145**

The wonder of creation 146

Stewardship of the world. 153

Litanies **155**

The Church **165**

The local church 166

Vocations in the Church 172

Discipleship and mission. 178

Baptism, marriage and funerals 189

Saints and Seasons. **193**

Advent 194

Christmas 198

Epiphany 200

Lent and Passiontide 202

Easter 207

Other festivals. 211

Saints' Days 214

Index: numerical **233**

Index: alphabetical. **253**

Preface: Prayers for private and public worship

For thirteen years, I shared with colleagues in the Durham Cathedral Chapter the joy and privilege of leading the intercessions each day at Morning Prayer and Evensong. We all put great care into the preparation of the intercessions and frequently we were asked after the service where people could obtain a copy of the prayers we had used because, as one person said to me, "You put into words what I want to say to God." Some people expressed surprise that prayers could be so relevant to what was happening in the world.

Whilst I drew on the rich resources of Christian prayer through the ages, I also wrote many prayers myself and kept them in a computer file. They were the starting point for this book, supplemented by others, many of which were written during the COVID-19 lockdowns. The ideas for the prayers came from whatever was in the news on the day of writing, from continuing prayer concerns and from the needs and situations of people on my personal prayer list. The thematic range is wide, but I make no claim for it to be comprehensive, and where there are omissions, I hope these prayers will inspire people to write their own. All the prayers can be used in personal prayer but are also written for public worship and therefore there are no personal references; many, however, began with a particular situation in mind as I prayed for someone I knew or asked myself how I might lead people in public prayer around a particular issue or current news event.

Leading prayer in public worship is not the same as praying on one's own or in a small prayer group with friends or family. For a start, the prayers are part of a bigger liturgy and need to fit into that, neither suddenly dragging prayer off in an entirely new direction nor simply repeating what has already been said or sung. The language of the prayers should not jar with the language of the rest of the service: at the Cathedral, where Morning Prayer was from *Common Worship* and Evensong from the *Book of Common Prayer*, there were subtle differences in the ways we prayed at the two services. This was probably unnoticed by most people because the prayers blended seamlessly into the liturgy, whereas people would have noticed and perhaps been jolted by the language if it did not fit with the overall tone of the service.

The prayers are the corporate prayers of the gathered body of Christ so need to be something people can own for themselves and thus say "Amen" to with integrity. Unlike the fixed parts of the liturgy, people do not know what is coming next so the intention of the prayers must be instantly clear and appropriate for a mixed gathering. There are ways to pray at times of parliamentary elections, for example, which can be shared by people whose political persuasions differ, just as there are ways not to pray in public at such times. On the other hand, there are times when prayer must be prophetic if it is to honour God and care for people in need. Finding the appropriate balance between being prophetic and being wrongly nationalistic or party political can require careful thought before pen is put to paper, or finger to keyboard. Perhaps obviously, but it needs to be said, public prayer is nearly always best expressed in the first person plural, not the first person singular, because in leading public prayers we are inviting others to join us in prayer, not to overhear our personal prayer time. We probably all have memories of services where, for one reason or another, the prayers were not those of the gathered people in which we could join: I recall a wedding where several friends of the bride and groom came forward to pray but had obviously not prepared or discussed their prayers beforehand, so the congregation overheard almost identical impromptu personal prayers, each beginning with and then being punctuated regularly by the phrase "I just want to pray that . . .". Although heartfelt personal prayers, they felt exclusive in public worship and were unnecessarily repetitive. As someone once commented wryly, "The prayers of the just can be very tedious." So the prayers in this book use the "we" form of wording and, while this can be adapted to "I" in personal prayer, there is something powerful about praying "we" even when we are on our own because doing so acts as a reminder that when we pray we are always joining with the worldwide Church of God on earth and with (as the liturgy puts it so vividly) "angels, archangels and all the company of heaven".

When leading the intercessions during Evensong at the Cathedral, we included three or four prayers—for the Church, the world, people in need and one other theme, perhaps creation, thanksgiving, an evening prayer or for a particular situation not covered elsewhere. This might be an event in the Cathedral earlier in the day or something suggested by one of the psalms or readings or by the 5 o'clock news which I always checked before leaving for the cathedral if I was leading the intercessions. Four prayers was not a hard-and-fast rule but useful as a benchmark. The prayers in this book are of varying lengths, usually between about 60 and 120 words, so, with the acoustics of Durham Cathedral's particular physical space and sound system, four prayers would take about four to five minutes. Churches differ, so it is worth timing how many words a minute are audible at the back of the church where you lead prayers and keep that as your benchmark.

One of the reasons for the ongoing love of the *Book of Common Prayer* is that Thomas Cranmer knew how to write a good prayer, both in terms of structure and language. The Collect form of prayer, which he used frequently, has proven its worth as a succinct way of praying and many of the prayers in this book follow it (more or less). A Collect, which "collects" the prayers of the people, has the basic structure of an address to God ("Almighty God"), a statement of some attribute of God on which the prayer that follows is predicated ("who seest that we have no power of ourselves to help ourselves"); a petition ("Keep us both outwardly in our bodies and inwardly in our souls"); the desired outcome of the petition ("that we may be defended from all adversities which may happen to the body, and from all evil thoughts which may assault and hurt the soul"); and the basis of our confidence in praying ("through Jesus Christ our Lord. Amen"). While that example, Cranmer's Collect for the Second Sunday in Lent, follows the structure, in some cases the order may be varied: the petition or the desired outcome may come first. All prayers should indicate to whom they are prayed, otherwise they are simply vague hopes not addressed to anyone in particular.

The rhythm of language is important when leading public worship: the prayer should flow and so, once the theme of the prayer is determined, attention should be given to which words will best express it, which in turn means attention both to nuances of meaning and to syllables and stress. I frequently use the thesaurus facility on the computer to check if there is an alternative way of saying something that will flow more easily. Think, too, of Cranmer's innate sense of how repetition or related phrases can add beauty and dignity to prayers: "devices and desires"; "to whom all hearts are open, all desires known, and from whom no secrets are hid"; "and are heartily sorry for these our misdoings, the remembrance of them is grievous unto us, the burden of them is intolerable". On the other hand, there can be too much loaded into one prayer, too many adjectives or adverbs, or words that don't flow, so it is always wise to listen to yourself praying the prayer out loud in private before doing so in public.

Public prayer only has integrity if it grows out of personal prayer: people will know if it does not. I hope that these prayers are a resource for all who pray, whether in private or in public.

The Revd Canon Rosalind Brown
Holy Week 2021

THE NEEDS OF THE WORLD

General world needs

1. Inexpressible need

Lord, when we have no words for our world's need,
we bring our muteness and pray once again, "Lord, open our lips";
when despair is best expressed in tears,
we bring our fragile hope on behalf of a weeping world;
when we cannot see beyond the moment,
we pray for hope that sees through the horizon;*
when we barely dare to dream,
stop us in our tracks
and remind us of the fidelity that lies in hopeful living;
Lord, give us the strenuous hope to act faithfully
for a world so often paralysed by despair. Amen.

2. Response to suffering

O holy God,
when the suffering in the news
is beyond our power to comprehend
and overwhelms us into numbness,
break through our paralysis and show us what we can do
to facilitate relief that others are better placed to deliver,
to influence our own nation's response to needs here or overseas,
and to assist with action where we can make a difference.
*Particularly today we pray for the people of . . . / devastated by
    . . . and for the relief efforts being made even as we pray.*
We pray this in the name of Jesus Christ our Lord. Amen.

---

*   In Indonesian the word for "hope" apparently means "to see through the horizon".

3. Extreme horrors

When our senses are numbed with horror on an industrial scale,
when we walk helplessly the corridors of other people's suffering,
or are haunted by stories beyond our comprehension,
then come, O Lord, with your peace
and show us how to bring new hope amidst the darkness
    of our shared and sometimes dishonourable history.
In your name we pray. Amen.

4. Good citizenship

As we pray for our world, O Lord,
in all its beauty and desolation,
we pray that you will stab our consciences,
so that we live with love and respect for your natural creation,
for the diversity of peoples made in your image,
and for the cultures of all nations.
Give us wisdom and teachability in our citizenship,
so that we live with a wider perspective on your ways
    for the world than those of nationalism and self-interest,
and make us agents of change for the good of all.
In the name of Jesus Christ we pray. Amen.

5. Building a righteous world

Lord God, our creator and our judge,
in times when our deepest allegiances are tested
by the conflicting demands of a complex world,
we pray that we may be found faithful
in our thoughts, words and actions,
so that we may play our part in building a world
where righteousness shines
and party-spirit, selfishness and hatred are replaced
    by generosity and compassion.
In the name of Jesus Christ our Lord. Amen.

6. People in today's news

O Lord God,

when we follow the news

    and see how life is soured by sin and selfishness,

we are shamed by the unnecessary suffering of others

and the appalling actions that deny our common humanity.

As we pray for the people caught up in the horrors of today's news,

especially . . .

we pray for forgiveness for the times when our own actions,

less dramatic but still harmful,

have contributed to the diminishment of your world.

O holy God, hear our cry for the wellbeing of all peoples and nations

and the healing of the hurts we so callously inflict on one another.

We pray in the name of Jesus Christ our Lord. Amen.

7. The victims of tragedy or terror

When we look at photos, taken in happy times,

of people in the news who are united only by being

    the victims of another atrocity, of brutality or terror,

we find it hard to comprehend their cruel loss.

Hear us as we pray in silence for the people who knew and loved

the people behind the haunting images.

In their profound loss, dear Lord, gently wipe away their tears.

Keep us, O Lord, prayerful for all of them over the coming days.

In the name of Jesus Christ our Lord. Amen.

People with power or influence in the world

8. International relations

Deliver us, O God, as a nation and world
from the obsession with instant results,
the search for someone to blame,
and the tyranny of unrestrained self-interest.
Teach us to be trustworthy in fulfilling our own responsibilities,
generous in our acceptance of the best efforts of others,
and honest in our search for what is best for all people in your world.
We pray in the name of Jesus Christ,
who was willing to lay aside the protection of his own reputation
and to give his life in the service of others. Amen.

9. International relations

O Lord, when international relations are tense,
bring patience and good diplomacy;
when there is fear of war or internal dispute,
bring peace-making and a considered response;
when there is unrest, mistrust or antagonism,
bring calm and an understanding of other points of view;
and where there is a threat of dangerous or irresponsible action,
stay the hand of those involved.
Inspire our world leaders with new commitment to peace and goodwill,
and raise their vision and actions beyond self-interest
to a commitment to seek the welfare of all peoples and nations.
We pray this for the wellbeing of your world. Amen.

10. The United Nations and international organizations
In a world where international cooperation
is so essential to our mutual wellbeing,
we pray for the work of the United Nations
and other international organizations.
Teach us, O Lord, to value collaboration more deeply
and to commit ourselves to the demanding path
   of understanding and cooperation
that transcends nationalist self-interests and remembered hatreds.
We pray for all people who work in the public eye
   or behind the scenes to build trust between nations and peoples.
We pray this for the wellbeing of the world
which you have entrusted to our stewardship.
In the name of Jesus Christ our Lord. Amen.

11. The United Nations
In times *(this time)* of international tension(s),
we pray for the work of the United Nations and other agencies
   that promote international understanding and collaboration.
Guide us together into the ways of peace,
and bless all who work patiently to establish the mutual trust
that can enable progress towards the resolution of conflicts.
We pray especially for people working to bring peace to . . .
We pray this in the name of Jesus Christ, the Prince of Peace. Amen.

12. World leaders

Protect the world, O Lord, we pray,
from people who have power or influence
   and are freer with their words and ideologies
   instead of the wisdom the world so desperately needs.
We ask that you would raise up leaders in the nations
   who have the humility to recognize their limits
   and to seek sound counsel and advice.
We pray this in the name of Jesus Christ. Amen.

13. World leaders

We pray, O Lord, for world leaders,
those who have been given authority and those who have taken power.
May their ambitions be selfless,
their motives honourable,
their vision compassionate,
their thinking wise,
their actions appropriate,
and their authority exercised for the wellbeing of all people.
We ask this through Jesus Christ our Lord. Amen.

14. World leaders

Lord, you put down the mighty from their seats
and exalt the humble and meek:
we pray for leaders of the world,
however they inflate or underestimate themselves,
guide them in their leadership,
give them wisdom in difficult situations,
restrain their dangerous thoughts and actions
and prosper their life-bringing work.
We pray this in the name of the Prince of Peace. Amen.

15. World leaders

We pray, almighty God,
for healthy relationships between leaders of nations.
We pray that relationships of trust will be built
    which respect each other's human dignity
without necessarily condoning each other's actions.
When world leaders tread that difficult path
between the particular interests of their nations and peoples
and ensuring the wellbeing of your whole world,
help them to find a balance that reflects your justice and your mercy,
to have the courage to oppose injustice and oppression
while continuing to negotiate for reconciliation and peace,
and to learn to disagree constructively.
As we pray for them to be peacemakers for the good of your world,
so we pray the same for ourselves in our own, more local situations.
We ask this in the name of Jesus Christ, the Prince of Peace. Amen.

16. World leaders and armed forces at times of tension

Deliver your world, O holy God,
from the desire for revenge and from the rage and blame-laying
    that underlie so much of international relations.
Guide the leaders of the nations into the ways of justice and peace,
and deliver them and us from the powerful grip of the unrestrained ego.
Where military intervention is needed,
we pray for its wise and restrained use,
and for all who serve in the armed forces of their countries
    in such times.
Draw us all to the self-giving love of the cross,
that it may be the exemplar for peoples and nations.
In the name of Jesus Christ,
who bore that cross
to save the world from its sin and shame. Amen.

17. International or national crises

Lord Jesus, you faced volatile situations:
we pray for people with influence who, today, feel fearful and confused,
or who are struggling to know what to think and do.
We pray especially for politicians and military leaders
facing situations that are beyond their previous
     experience or competence,
and where unwise action could exacerbate tense situations:
help them not to overreact, but to think with clarity and wise insight,
give them the courage to take patient, slow steps
towards solutions that contribute to the wellbeing of all your world.
We pray this in your name, O Prince of Peace. Amen.

18. Integrity in public life

We pray, O God, for integrity in the corridors of power
     and in the alleys of backstreet life:
for all with power over others that can be used for good or ill,
for all who control or manipulate financial and other resources,
for all who can give or withhold what is needful for others to flourish,
for all who hold the power of life and death,
and for all who have a measure of control that can be used selfishly
     or for the wellbeing of others.
O holy God, where power is corrupted, curtail its influence,
and where power is used wisely,
grant that it may prosper the wellbeing of your people.
In the name of Jesus Christ our Lord. Amen.

19. Sound advice and just action
In a world which craves slick answers and quick results,
we pray that the leaders of the nations of the world
    will turn to sound advisers,
have the insight to discern what is not merely expedient but right,
and the courage to follow just courses of action
    for the good of all people,
especially the poor and overlooked.
We pray this in the name of Jesus Christ
the Prince of Peace. Amen.

20. Integrity in the media and communications
O holy God,
we pray for integrity in our national press and in social media.
Deliver us from deceptive headlines, knee-jerk reactions and half-truths
and from the nastiness of slander and traducement.
Show us how to communicate wisely and honestly,
so that truth is not sacrificed to opportunism or party spirit.
We pray, too, for young people whose lives
    are blighted by online bullying.
We thank you for all the benefits of modern communication,
and pray that we will be good stewards of the opportunities it presents
to work for the good of all people in our society.
In the name of Jesus Christ our Lord. Amen.

Justice and wellbeing for all

21. Justice
Let justice roll on earth, we pray.
Lord, bring new hope to birth,
teach us to recognize injustice and its lies,
tune our hearts to hear the cries of broken hearts,
and enlarge our resolve to be agents of your jubilee,
proclaiming liberty to captives and seeking dignity for all people.
Let justice roll on earth. Amen.

22. Acting for justice
Where there is hatred in the world
challenge us to act with love.
Where there is abuse in the world,
stir us to work for its abolition.
Where there is discrimination in the world,
remind us that we are all equal in your sight,
and where there is injustice in the world
fire us with passion for righteousness to prevail.
O Lord our God, may our lives increasingly express
your good purposes for all peoples. Amen.

23. Justice
Rekindle in your people, O Lord,
a sense of justice that is not swayed by expediency,
and the commitment to work for people
who yearn for someone to stand up for them.
We pray this in the name of Jesus Christ our Lord. Amen.

24. Peace and justice for all

As we dream of a world which reflects your good purposes
yet grieve at the suffering and injustice that pervades its life,
we pray, O God our Creator and Lord,
for the protection of the poor and weak,
for the sharing of resources essential for daily life,
and for the establishment of peace and justice
in places of war and hatred.
May all peoples around the world
know themselves cared for and valued.
We ask this in the name of Jesus Christ our Lord. Amen.

25. People living with injustice

O heavenly Father, in your mercy,
protect people who today face injustice
with no resources to contest it or defend their human rights.
Bless them in their isolation and fear
and prosper the work of Amnesty International and other organizations
which challenge corruption and the abuse of power.
We pray this in the name of Jesus Christ our Lord. Amen.

26. Powerlessness

Lord Jesus, you did not resist when you were arrested and bound,
and you know what it is to be given over to the power of others:
we pray for vulnerable people who are at the mercy of others,
especially those in the hands of cruel people
who have no awareness of justice and compassion.
Be alongside those who suffer, Lord Jesus,
and fire our commitment to work for their relief and wellbeing.
We pray this in your name, Lord Jesus. Amen.

27. World inequality

In a world of inequality,
where need and suffering transcend political and racial boundaries,
we pray that you will lead the nations into the risky give-and-take
     of equality for the wellbeing of all your people.
In the name of Jesus Christ our Lord. Amen.

28. Valuing difference

Lord Jesus, you chose radically different people to be your close friends
and invited them to learn to work, travel and relax together:
we ask for an increasing delight in the differences
     we experience in each other.
Teach us to rejoice in the many ways we express God's image in us;
lead us across the divisions of race, gender, culture, sexuality,
     nationality, language, education and interests;
and excite us with the possibilities of growing together in love.
We pray too for the breaking down of barriers
     between peoples and nations
and an increase in the appreciation of the gifts we can offer each other.
We pray this in the name of Jesus Christ our Lord. Amen.

29. Fairness in international trade

In a world so dependent on international trade and supply lines,
we pray for all who have to make difficult decisions
     about the allocation of needed resources,
for all who manage the logistics and practicalities of distribution,
and for nations that cannot compete on equal terms
     due to a lack of resources or political instability.
When we feel powerless to help,
     show us what we can do to influence the patterns of world trade
for the good of all peoples and not just national self-interests.
In the name of Jesus Christ our Lord. Amen.

War and peace

30. Broken dreams

O holy God, when our dreams of a world of peace,
of justice and freedom for all,
lie shattered in a city's rubble,
streak through the air in a missile;
or gaze at us through the dulled eyes of a refugee,
rekindle our fading hopes to pray
for your kingdom of peace and justice to be known in all the earth.
We pray in the name of Jesus Christ, the Prince of Peace. Amen.

31. An end to war

Amidst the landscapes made desolate by war,
we pray for all who work to bring an end to hatred and to strife.
O Prince of Peace,
guide the hearts and minds of world leaders
to pursue peace and reconciliation.
Strengthen the hands that work to bring reconciling love
to places of degradation and despair,
and give us all the determination to dare to build
a world of justice and of grace. Amen.

32. The victims of war

We hold before you, O Lord,
all who are caught up in the tragedies of wars
that are not of their making,
all who are at the mercy of aggressors
who use war as a cover for vindictiveness,
all who are victims of blind obedience
    to corrupt and evil dogmas and regimes.
Heavenly Father, as you see the single sparrow that falls to the ground,
we pray your protection for the unnoticed victims of our wars and conflicts.
We pray this in the name of Jesus Christ our Lord. Amen.

33. Long-standing enmity

We pray for the resolution of enmity between peoples and nations
which has existed for reasons now forgotten but never forgiven.
O God, break the power and grip of memories
that cannot let go of the fears that underlie so many hatreds,
and in their place sow seeds of your reign of love and peace.
Teach us to tend and water those gardens of improbable hope.
In the name of Jesus Christ our Lord. Amen.

34. War crimes

Bring the light of your holiness, O Lord,
to the many outrages of war,
and to the crimes against humanity
that demean and abuse the victims and destroy human dignity.
We pray for today's victims of genocide and war crimes
    who still await deliverance,
victims of past war crimes who still bear the scars of their suffering,
and all who work to bring the perpetrators to justice.
Prosper the work of the International Criminal Court
and all who work tirelessly to restore the health of people whose
    lives have been devastated by the hatred of others.
We pray this for the sake of Jesus Christ our Lord. Amen.

35. Terrorism and horrendous evil

In the face of horrendous evil and wilfully inflicted suffering
  beyond our comprehension, we pray, O Lord,
with confused thoughts rather than our coherent words.
We pray for those who suffer or are bereaved
  through the cruelty of others,
for all involved in bringing emergency responses,
for those who nurse and care for the injured,
and all who will work in the long term
to ease the ongoing trauma of those who have suffered.
Especially we pray for . . .
Since Jesus taught us to pray for our enemies we pray, too,
for the people who have inflicted these horrors,
asking that they will be turned from their wicked ways
towards compassion for peoples of all nationalities, races and faiths.
We pray in the name of Jesus Christ our Lord. Amen.

36. Being peacemakers

Make us, O Lord, into peacemakers wherever you place us.
We pray for people with power and influence in the affairs of the world,
that they may never abuse the privilege entrusted to them;
we pray for people of harsh ideologies and no concept of compassion,
that they may be challenged by the horror of
  their own implacable beliefs;
we pray for armed forces of the nations and for unofficial militias,
that they will serve with discipline
and protect the vulnerable whom they encounter;
we pray for people with hearts set to serve
  the victims of hatred and cruelty,
that they will shine as lights in the darkness where sin and suffering rule;
and we pray for ourselves, who feel powerless
  to change the world for good,
that we will know how best to act and pray in our corner of it.
Make us, O Lord, into peacemakers wherever you place us. Amen.

37. Peaceful life in cities

Lord Jesus Christ,
you wept over the city of Jerusalem and its refusal of your peace:
we pray for the peaceful life of cities *(especially ...)*
that their peoples of many races and faiths may live together in joy
and without rancour or fear;
that their political and religious leaders
may find common ground in their pursuit of peace and justice;
and that life in our cities will become a beacon of hope
for all the nations of the world.
We ask this in your name, O Prince of Peace. Amen.

38. Peace

Guide our footsteps, O God our Good Shepherd, into the paths of peace,
turn us from hatreds that tend to war,
from fears that tend to aggression,
from desires that tend to greed for other people's goods.
Help us to be builders and keepers of peace. Amen.

Refugees and people in danger

39. Refugees

Lord Jesus, you were a refugee as a baby:
we pray for all who are refugees today:
for families in refugee camps
or trudging on dangerous journeys,
for parents who despair at being unable to provide for their children,
for children who have been separated from their parents,
and for older people and those with physical challenges,
whose needs go unmet.
Keep them safe from harm and exploitation,
and enable them to find shelter, food and a caring welcome.
In your name we pray, Amen.

40. Refugees

Protect, O Lord, refugees who, even as we pray,
face the dangers and insecurities of life on the road
    or inadequate shelter in overcrowded refugee camps.
We pray for parents trying to protect their children
    while lacking the basic necessities of life,
for older people who find the rigours of travel hard
    and whose medical needs go unmet,
and for children travelling alone,
relying on their wits and the goodwill of others.
In their exhaustion, Lord, may they find refreshment,
in their fears may they find people to support them,
and in their dangers may they be kept from harm.
We pray this in the name of Jesus Christ our Lord. Amen.

41. Refugees

For refugees in crowded and insanitary camps,
for people tramping through rain and cold, drought and heat
to reach a place of safety and new hope,
for children separated from their parents and carers
and living at the mercy of whoever they meet on the road,
for all who are living with the loss of their homeland and security,
and for all people seeking to give them dignity
    and safety in their troubled times,
we pray, O loving God. Amen.

42. Children separated from their families

We pray for children who are separated from their families
and long to be reunited,
for children who have no recollection of family life
    or experience of loving and being loved,
for children who fend for themselves on the streets or in gangs,
and who face violence on a daily basis,
for children conscripted as child soldiers or slaves of soldiers,
trafficked or kept as prostitutes,
and who live with abuse or exploitation.
For all these children, O heavenly Father, we ask your protection,
and pray that you will prosper the work of people
    and agencies working to secure their freedom
and ensure that their rights as children are met.
We pray this in the name of your Son,
who knew the insecurity of life as a refugee
as well as the joy of a nurturing family. Amen.

43. People who suffer

We pray, O Lord, for people who suffer
from war or conflict,
from economic or social poverty,
from hate crime or unequal opportunities,
from abuse or domestic violence,
from natural or human-made disaster,
from homelessness or lack of educational opportunity.
Forgive our indifference
and show us what we can do
to relieve need on our doorstep or around the world.
We pray this in the name of Jesus Christ our Lord. Amen.

44. People in danger

Holy and compassionate God, our Good Shepherd,
we pray for people trapped
in the depths of the dereliction and dangers of this world,
those in the frontline of other people's wars,
refugees on dangerous journeys or in camps
    with no shelter or place of safety,
vulnerable children and people who have been trafficked,
who cannot escape their abusers,
victims of domestic violence, racial, sexual or xenophobic hatred,
people with addictions, especially those who sleep on our streets,
and all for whom the world is a harsh and hostile place.
Look with mercy on them in their desolation,
guide those who provide support and care,
and inspire us to offer our resources for their wellbeing.
In the name of Jesus Christ our Lord, Amen.

45. People who have lost hope of relief

Heal, O gentle God,
the aches of those who carry sadness in their bones
    and cannot find relief.
We pray for people in countries where war or
    suffering are the only landscape for living,
and for people who no longer have a country to call their home
    but are haunted by memories of a past that is forever lost.
Succour and strengthen them,
and grant them a place of safety in which to make a home
and build new lives of hope.
We pray this in the name of Jesus Christ,
who at times had nowhere to lay his head. Amen.

46. Forgotten news headlines

Shock us, Lord God, with our ability to forget so quickly
    the headlines which shocked us so recently.
We pray for places of disaster, tragedy or war
that filled the media and stirred our emotions
but now elude our attention,
especially . . .
We pray for people engaged in the painstakingly slow work
of rescue, repair and restoration to remedy destruction,
for staff of charities and governments
negotiating the red tape and logistics of supply chains,
for medical staff caring for the sick and dying in hospitals
    with inadequate equipment or in the line of danger,
and for the people who still wait for rescue to come.
We pray this in the name of Jesus Christ, who brought
    healing and restoration to people he met. Amen.

47. People who have lost their freedom
Lord Jesus, you called Matthew from his lonely life
benefiting from the corrupt Roman tax system
and transformed him into your friend and disciple.
We pray for all who are trapped in the deprivations
    and injustices of corrupt living,
for the victims of human trafficking and slavery,
of substance addiction, prostitution and money laundering,
and for child soldiers, political prisoners and gang members.
Deliver them, we pray, from the grip of corruption
and liberate them from all that binds them,
so that they find the freedom that Matthew came to know.
Give courage, resilience and success to people
who work to break the power of society's sin and evil,
and to detect and restrain the perpetrators and beneficiaries
of the diminishment of other people.
So bring us all into fullness of life
in and through our Lord Jesus Christ. Amen.

48. The aftermath of oppression
We pray for people who live with the aftermath
    of cruelty and oppression:
for nations that have overthrown corrupt governments
and seek to build a healthy common life for their people,
for nations where the powerful have been fed
while famine has destroyed people, animals and crops,
leaving survivors dependent on unreliable aid,
for nations where oppressive regimes have imprisoned or silenced
    any voices that dared to speak out or to challenge them,
and the tyrannized who are too dispirited
    to take the initiative themselves.
For all these people, and for those still enduring such oppressive conditions,
we pray for freedom and release.
In the name of Jesus Christ,
whose mother sang of the mighty being put down from their seats. Amen.

49. People who are oppressed

Lord Jesus Christ, you acted with compassion
when you met people who were oppressed:
we pray for people whose lives have been devastated
    by the actions and attitudes of others:
for those who have been conditioned to think themselves worthless,
    had their individuality silenced,
been forced into work that demeans, debases or destroys,
or been subjected to mental or physical abuse.
We pray for rescue and release for those still trapped in these evils
    and courage for those working towards freedom
    from the lingering consequences.
May they find a new voice that can express their name
    with dignity and delight.
We pray this in your name, O Lord. Amen.

50. People who lack the essentials of life

As we pray for people in need around the world,
we remember in particular people whose needs
    are unglamorous but pervasive.
Especially we pray for people who cannot maintain the basic standards
    of hygiene and health that we take for granted,
for those who do not have access to clean water,
soap, disinfectants or personal hygiene items,
for people whose diets are inadequate, monotonous
    or lacking in essential vitamins;
for people who breathe polluted air or never see the sun,
or who have nowhere safe to sleep.
As we pray for all people who lack the basic essentials of life,
we ask that you will stir our consciences
and show us how to play our part in sharing the resources of your world.
We pray in the name of Jesus Christ our Lord. Amen.

51. Walking

When we enjoy going for a walk,
remind us, O Lord, of people for whom walking
    is a matter of life and death.
We pray for people who have to walk long distances,
often with inadequate footwear or in intolerable heat or cold,
to find security and safety, clean water, education or work.
Protect them from danger, O Lord,
and, when their walking becomes trudging or limping,
we pray that they will find people to provide refreshment
and the help they need to reach their destination.
We remember, Lord Jesus, that you both enjoyed and endured walking
and we pray this in your name. Amen.

52. Suffering that is no longer in the news

God of this uncertain world,
you sent Jesus to bring comfort and good news
    to the troubled and the suffering:
look with compassion on the people
    whose lives have been shattered *by . . .*
and by disasters which were once in the headlines
yet, though now far from our attention, still wreak desolation.
We pray for healing for the injured,
comfort for the bereaved,
strength and compassion for those who care for them,
and wisdom and skill for those who work to restore order and stability.
We ask your consolation for all who are frightened
    or bewildered by what they have experienced.
In their confusion and despair
may they turn to you for solace
and hold fast to your promise of refuge and strength. Amen.

53. Rain

Christopher Robin* didn't care if it rained,
but we pray for all to whom rain does matter:
for the people who welcome the rain
to water parched fields and gardens,
and to fill empty wells and reservoirs,
for the people who do not want it to rain,
fearing floods,
damage to property and livelihoods,
or the spread of disease.
We pray too for people who work outdoors whatever the weather,
or who sleep on the streets and have no shelter.
*We remember particularly today people in . . . who are struggling to cope
with the drought / the rain that has fallen.*
Lord Jesus, you were often out in all weathers,
bless and protect people today who are caught in the rain.
In your name we pray. Amen.

54. Water supplies

We pray, our Father,
for people living with too much water or too little water:
for those whose life is disrupted by flooding,
and for those facing prolonged drought.
We pray, too, for people who long for clean water to drink
and an end to water-borne diseases,
and for people who make tiring treks to collect water day by day.
Forgive us for our actions which contribute to floods or droughts,
and inspire us to work to ensure reliable supplies
of clean water for all your people.
We pray this in the name of Jesus Christ our Lord. Amen.

---

* See the poem "The Engineer" by A. A. Milne

Disasters

55. Our response to disaster

O Lord, as we hear of yet another disaster,
stir us to prayer and generosity.
Remind us that, although the problem may be far from us,
it is close at hand for the people affected,
and close to your heart of compassion for your world.
Deliver us from the complacency of hiding
    behind platitudes or statistics,
and teach us to pray with imagination and compassion
    for the people who suffer.
We pray for organizations working to provide emergency aid,
and for the logistics of delivering it.
All this we ask in the name of Jesus Christ. Amen.

56. People affected by natural disaster

When natural disaster strikes and life becomes a nightmare
from which there is no waking up,
we yearn, O Lord, for an end to the suffering.
We pray for people *especially* . . .
for whom there can be no instant relief
    or assurance of long-term recovery.
When they are numbed, exhausted or paralysed into inaction,
give them the strength to do what little they can.
Where there is no safe ground on which to wait for rescue,
protect them from danger,
and, if they have been separated from family and friends,
bring them the consolation that passes all human understanding.
Speed and prosper the work of emergency relief teams
and the provision of long-term assistance to restore ordered life.
We pray this in the name of Jesus Christ our Lord. Amen.

57. Disaster

When disaster strikes,
be present, O Lord, our Good Shepherd,
to bring comfort, relief, shelter and human kindness.
Shield the people who suffer,
prosper the provision of relief,
and shine your light and hope into the midst of despair.
We pray this in the name of Jesus Christ,
the Good Shepherd. Amen.

58. Pandemic

When a pandemic faces us with crisis, O God,
help us to not just react to imminent problems
    but to embrace long-term opportunities.
Guide our responses to the immediate needs
    of all who are sick and vulnerable,
and the need for resources for frontline services.
But guide us too, O God, in our responses
to the challenges to our future way of life:
show us what has to change
if we are to prevent this from happening again,
and the opportunities this crisis presents
to live differently in the years to come
as better stewards of your world.
O Lord, guide us through the confusion of the present time
to a healthier and more faithful lifestyle for all nations and peoples.
We pray in the name of Jesus Christ our Lord. Amen.

59. Epidemic or pandemic

When an epidemic or pandemic disrupts our lives
and forces us to live with fear and uncertainty,
we pray that you will keep us steady in our living,
wise in our actions
and compassionate in our response to people who suffer.
Guide the people
who have responsibility for making the difficult
   decisions needed for our corporate wellbeing.
Prosper the work of research scientists
who seek answers to hitherto unknown dilemmas,
and sustain all who care for the sick
and people whose lives have been devastated.
We pray this in the name of Jesus Christ our Lord. Amen.

60. Major accident

In an age when travel is so vital to our way of life,
we hear with shock and sorrow of *the plane /*
   train crash / major accident . . . ,
knowing how easily we could have been the passengers.
We pray, O Lord, for everyone affected:
the injured and shocked,
the emergency services
and all involved in the rescue efforts,
and the hospitals which will receive the injured.
We pray too for families and friends who wait fearfully for news,
and for those who already know that they are bereaved.
In our shared sadness make your compassionate presence known,
and shield those most directly affected with your love and mercy.
Bless the people who will clear the debris,
investigate the cause of the accident,
and work to increase safety for all who travel.
We pray this in the name of Jesus Christ. Amen.

61. Forest fires

Where forest fires burn out of control,
we pray, Lord God,
for the safety of people and wildlife caught in their path,
and for skill and success for firefighters, emergency and support services.
Where people's homes and livelihoods are destroyed,
we pray for the provision of immediate relief and help
and support in the laborious process of long-term recovery.
Where the fires are caused by reckless actions
or mismanagement of the natural environment,
challenge governments and individuals
about careless or selfish ways of life,
and provoke in us all the will to restore an appropriate balance
between humanity and the natural world.
We pray this in sorrow for our exploitation of your world,
O Lord our God. Amen.

Rescue, emergency and aid workers

62. Relief workers

Compassionate God,
we thank you for the dedication and bravery of relief and aid workers.
Protect them from harm when they are in dangerous conditions,
inspire them with hope when they are overwhelmed by the needs
with which they are faced,
and give them the skill and creativity to respond in situations
that stretch them to the limit.
We pray this in the name of Jesus Christ,
who reached out to help people in need. Amen.

63. People who risk their lives for others

O Prince of Peace,

we give thanks and pray for people who are willing

to risk their lives for the wellbeing of others.

Keep them safe,

prosper their caring work

and inspire others to train to join them.

We particularly remember

the people who detect and defuse land mines and unexploded bombs,

the rescue workers in . . . ,

the fire fighters in . . . ,

and our emergency and rescue services,

whether on land, sea or in the air.

Prosper their work and keep them safe, we pray. Amen.

NATIONAL AND LOCAL LIFE

Government and public life

64. Parliament

Guide, O Lord, the deliberations of our Parliament.
Grant wisdom to the people elected or appointed
    to serve the nation in government.
May there be a focus on all that is good and upright in national life,
an avoidance of rancour when discussions are difficult
    or conflicting interests are involved,
and a willingness to work together across party lines
    for the welfare and prosperity of all people.
We pray for the Prime Minister,
the Leader of the Opposition,
members of their cabinets,
and for all constituency MPs
and the people they serve.
May we be a nation known for integrity
in our institutions of government.
We pray this in the name of Jesus Christ our Lord. Amen.

65. Administration of government

Give wisdom, we pray, O Lord,
to all who work in the administration of government.
We pray for all people who advise ministers,
draft the details of legislation,
negotiate in complex situations,
and keep the administration of our nation's life running smoothly.
Prosper their work for the wellbeing of the nation.
We pray this in the name of Jesus Christ. Amen.

66. Integrity in public life

O holy God,
may there be integrity in the nation's corridors of power,
integrity in our civic life,
and integrity in our own daily actions and relationships.
We pray this in the name of Jesus Christ our Lord. Amen.

67. Financial constraint

In times of financial constraint,
give us all a due sense of what is most important in life.
Guide politicians and civil servants in the setting and
    balancing of budgets to which we all contribute.
Help them to hold in creative tension
    the endless needs yet limited resources,
and to make wise decisions about the allocation and administration
    of public money for the good of all members of our society.
Increase our generosity of spirit when we read our tax bill,
and make us wise stewards of the financial
    resources you have entrusted to us.
We pray in the name of Jesus Christ, who both paid his taxes
    and met the needs of people who turned to him. Amen.

68. Dissimulation in public life / Elections

In our national life, *especially at this time of national or local elections*,
we pray that you will protect us, O Lord,
from half-truths or convenient perspectives,
and duplicity in the presentation of information.
In a world of complex issues,
deliver us from contentment with slick answers
    and over-simplified assertions.
Help us as a nation to face the challenge of living with nuance,
probing carefully to find ethical rather than merely opportunistic
    approaches to issues of national importance.
We pray this in the name of Jesus Christ our Lord. Amen.

69. The Royal Family and the armed services

We pray, O Lord our God, for Her Majesty the Queen
and members of the Royal Family.
We give thanks for their examples of faithful and dutiful public service,
dedicated to the wellbeing of all peoples
    throughout the Commonwealth.
Refresh and renew them, we pray, in their daily responsibilities.
We pray, too, for the heads of our armed forces
and all who serve under them in the service of Queen and country:
may their decisions and action be wise and their example praiseworthy.
Together, may our contribution to the life of the world
be an exemplary and effective pursuit of peace and justice for all peoples.
We pray in the name of our Lord Jesus Christ. Amen.

National and local services

70. Unhealthy living environments

For children growing up in bleak urban areas, we pray, O Lord.
For those who lack access to unpolluted air,
who are surrounded by unattractive buildings and relentless noise,
who play in streets intended for traffic,
or who cannot leave a high-rise block in safety.
We pray for adequate provision of safe and accessible play space
to enable the healthy development which others take for granted.
We ask this in the name of Jesus Christ our Lord. Amen.

71. Children in cities

Protect the young people growing up in our cities, we pray,
from evils that insinuate themselves into their lives,
suck them into gangs, crime, addiction or prostitution,
and destroy the hope of a joyful, healthy life.
We pray for all youth workers in our inner cities,
especially those working as part of the mission of the Church.
We pray for the police, drug enforcement agencies,
    social services and probation services,
and for local communities in their response to needs in their area.
Prosper their work as agents of change
for the safety and wellbeing of the young people in our neighbourhoods.
We pray this in the name of Jesus Christ,
who transformed the lives of all he met. Amen.

72. Riots

When cities burn and anger spills onto the streets, O Lord,
may peace and justice prevail over chaos and fear.
We pray for all who are caught up in the violence *in* . . . ,
that the just needs and perspectives of people
whose anger or hopelessness leads them to fury will be heard,
that people who inflame unrest in order to serve other ends
will be restrained,
that those responsible for bringing an end to the violence
will act wisely, effectively and without further provocation,
and that people who have been injured or watch in fear
for their homes and livelihoods will find places of safety.
We pray, too, O Lord, that the longer-term response to the unrest
will further the reach of justice and equal opportunities
for all people.
We pray this in the name of Jesus Christ our Lord. Amen.

73. Damaged lives and unequal distribution of resources

In a world where what passes for love is too often unrecognizable
    compared to the touchstone of your expansive love for your world,
we pray, O holy God, for families and relationships
    where there is control, abuse or manipulation,
for communities where resources are hoarded selfishly
    or shared unequally,
for nations whose leaders are corrupted
by focusing on their own interests and security.
Into all these situations, breathe your life-giving Spirit,
and provide relief for people who are oppressed or overlooked.
We pray in the name of Jesus Christ our Lord. Amen.

74. Crime

We pray for all people who are affected by crime:
for its victims and people who live in fear of criminal activity,
its instigators and perpetrators,
and for young people who are sucked or coerced into gangs.
We pray for the police and courts,
prisoners and their families,
prison staff and after-care services,
and for probation staff and community service supervisors.
We pray too for released prisoners
as they seek to rebuild their lives outside prison.
Guide us to creative and purposeful responses
that make our neighbourhoods safer places for everyone.
Help those who work to reform our prisons be more effective
in dealing with offenders
and in equipping people for honest and productive living.
In the name of Jesus Christ our Lord. Amen.

75. Crime

Lord Jesus Christ,
your cousin and some of your disciples spent time in prison,
so we pray with confidence that you know the impact of imprisonment.
We pray for all people who are affected by crime,
especially people who are pushed to breaking point
by their own or a family member's imprisonment
or by the prolonged impact of being a victim of crime,
and for the people who provide mental health and welfare services.
In complex situations, we pray for clarity and compassion
    in the support that is offered to all affected by crime,
and we pray that the rehabilitation of offenders
will result in new beginnings of freedom and peace.
In your name we pray, O Lord. Amen.

76. Prisoners being released

We pray for prisoners who will be released today or in the near future,
and for families who anticipate their return
with joy, apprehension or dread.
For those who have no family to return to,
we pray that they will find a place to build a home and a new life,
and, for those in danger of slipping through the cracks
    in society's provision,
we pray for protection from harm to themselves or others
and access to the support they need
to establish a crime-free life in the future.
Strengthen the efforts of all who work
for the rehabilitation and care of ex-offenders,
and give wisdom to policy makers at national and local level.
In the name of Jesus Christ our Lord we pray. Amen.

77. Crime in the news

In our horror at the news of such callous crime
  that defies belief or understanding,
especially today's news of . . . ,
we pray for the victims,
their families and friends who will hear bad news,
for the emergency services and hospitals
  responding to immediate needs,
the police as they begin their investigations,
and for people who now live in fear
because crime has affected their neighbourhood.
We pray, too, for the perpetrator(s)
that they will turn from their wickedness
and face the justice that, through their actions,
  they have brought on themselves.
O holy God, we pray this in the name of Jesus Christ our Lord. Amen.

78. Murder

O Lord, when we are shocked by the horror of murder,
lead us all into paths of righteous living.
We pray for those who are traumatized,
for the families and friends of the person murdered,
for people who are haunted by what they have seen or experienced,
for the police in their detection of the crime,
the prison service in its oversight of those arrested,
the Crown Prosecution Service in its pursuit of justice,
and the person or people responsible for this wickedness,
that they will have the courage to repent and amend their way of life.
Teach us as a society what it means to value people's lives,
when they can no longer speak for themselves.
We pray this in the name of Jesus Christ our Lord,
who was killed by others. Amen.

79. Homes that are dangerous

Protect, dear Lord, people who live in a place
that is not a home but a place fraught with danger.
Sharpen our response as a society to domestic violence and enslavement,
and prosper the work of the police and social service agencies
    in identifying and rescuing victims of violence in their homes.
We pray in the name of Jesus Christ our Lord. Amen.

80. Places of safety

We pray, O Lord, for all people who rely on safe houses:
for victims of domestic violence, human trafficking and slavery,
for unaccompanied child refugees,
people escaping from the control of gangs,
and for people in rehabilitation from addictions.
As we pray for their safety and wellbeing,
we pray as well for the people who provide places of safety,
and for politicians and administrators who make decisions
    that affect the resourcing of such facilities.
In demanding and complicated situations may the goal always be
the safety and wellbeing of those who are vulnerable,
rather than the political gains or losses that arise
from prioritizing these services.
In the name of Jesus Christ we pray. Amen.

81. Trauma in life

Almighty God, when our community or personal life is wrenched apart,
our illusions of order shattered,
and when havoc ruptures our sense of stability,
come to us amidst the earthquake, wind and fire,
and calm us to hear your still, small voice,
the sound of your sheer silence.
Help us to turn again and walk with you,
as our Lord Jesus Christ walked with his confused friends
on the Emmaus Road.
In his dear name we pray. Amen.

82. Addictions

Where addictions hold people in their power,
Lord, bring release to the captives.
Where addictions foster violence and destroy family life,
Lord, protect those who are vulnerable and distraught.
Where addictions fuel criminal activity,
Lord, empower the work of crime prevention and law enforcement.
Where addictions ruin lives,
Lord, bring new life and new beginnings.
We pray that the work of drug suppliers will be thwarted
and the work of addiction counsellors furthered,
in your name, Lord Jesus. Amen.

83. Addictions

Lord Jesus, you came to bring fullness of life for all people.
We pray for people who are trapped by addiction,
for their families and friends who watch in despair,
for counsellors and drug rehabilitation agencies,
and for the police and customs officers working to break supply lines.
We pray, too, for the people who produce or traffic drugs,
especially for young people who are controlled by gangs and drug lords.
Open to them new opportunities to break free from their bondage
and to find fullness of life in you.
We pray in your name. Amen.

84. Social Security and benefits

We pray, O God, for everyone involved in the Social Security system,
here desperate needs so often clash with official processes.
We pray for people who depend on benefits
and for people who determine or administer the benefit system.
We pray that this vital but complex system will work smoothly
to ensure that legitimate needs are identified and assessed properly,
resources go quickly where they are needed,
and fraud is rapidly detected.
Give patience and empathy to everyone involved,
we pray, Lord Jesus, in your name. Amen.

85. The misuse of resources

Forgive us, O God our Creator,
when we squander the resources you have entrusted to us:
the resources of the natural creation that we exploit or destroy,
the financial resources that we waste on unnecessary luxuries or trivia,
while millions starve or lack basic healthcare,
the friendships that we fail to cultivate or let circumstances undo,
the lives we allow to be devastated through neglect or cruelty.
We pray for forgiveness for our selfish ways of life.
Inspire us with new understandings of how we can play our small part
in living in more responsible and ethical ways.
We pray this for the good of your creation, O God. Amen.

86. The emergency services

We pray, O Lord God, for the police and emergency services
in their work to maintain order and provide rescue or help.
Bless their routine work and their responses to emergencies,
protect them from harm or danger,
and give them clarity of thought as they respond
to the demanding situations they face in the line of duty.
We give you thanks for their selfless service
    and the support offered by their families,
and we pray for people who are considering this work as a vocation.
In the name of Jesus Christ our Lord. Amen.

87. Undervalued workers

Teach us to value the contributions of people
who fulfil unglamorous but essential roles in our society,
and whose hard work so often goes unnoticed or taken for granted.
We pray for our care workers, street cleaners, public transport cleaners,
    rubbish collectors, delivery people and fruit pickers,
and all others who fulfil similar life-sustaining roles
and endure anti-social hours of work,
but often lack due recompense or job security.
Open our eyes, O Lord, to their contribution to our common life
and show us how to value their presence among us.
In the name of Jesus Christ our Lord. Amen.

88. Immigration policy

Lord God, who commanded your people to welcome
the needy and the stranger into their midst,
guide us as a nation
into righteous approaches to immigration policy and practice.
Unsettle and inspire us
with insights from the scriptures and from our history,
and free our eyes from blinkers to see with your eyes.
Guide our policy makers
into ways that establish the complex balance between
    the needs and aspirations of individuals and of our nation,
and, in our implementation of immigration policy,
make all our actions both humane and constructive
for the wellbeing of the people who want to move here.
We pray for them,
and pray all this in the name of Jesus Christ,
who, as a baby, was himself welcomed into the safety of another country.
Amen.

89. Industrial relations

Lead us, O Lord, as a nation,
into the practice of better industrial relations,
so that employers and employees
grow in appreciation of each other,
share common goals and seek each other's wellbeing.
(In this time of industrial unrest . . .)
We pray for union leaders and employers' organizations
as they negotiate fair employment agreements
    and safer working practices.
Where there is discontent,
show us all how to forge improved relationships
    that serve the common good.
Where redundancies loom,
guide the people who must make hard decisions
    that may adversely affect the lives of others.
And where strikes are threatened,
calm inflammatory responses and enable clarity
    in negotiations for the wellbeing of all people.
We pray in the name of Jesus Christ. Amen.

90. Farmers

In this season of harvest, we pray for all farmers and farm workers.
Prosper their work over the coming days, we pray.
We pray, too, for farmers around the world
who face poverty, hunger or bankruptcy
because their crops have been blighted, ruined or destroyed,
and for farmers facing low yields or low market prices.
Remind us all of our responsibility to care for your world,
and forgive us for our greedy exploitation of the soil.
Help us to find better ways of providing food
    for all the people of your world.
We pray in the name of Jesus Christ. Amen.

91. The media

Lord, we pray for everyone involved in the news media;
thank you for a free press and its potential for good.
We pray for all who work to bring the news to us each day:
protect journalists and their support teams
    who work in dangerous places,
give wisdom to news editors in their choice and wording of stories
and the courage to resist political manipulation or control,
protect us all from twisted truths and convenient lies,
and help us to read and listen with discernment and discretion.
We pray this for the wellbeing of your world
and in the name of Jesus Christ our Lord. Amen.

92. Facing adversity

Strengthen us, O Lord,
in our commitment to support and protect one another
as we face . . . *this threat* together.
We pray for people in the frontline of responses
    to the situation confronting us:
our political leaders in national and local government,
our emergency services, health and care workers,
our teachers and public service workers,
and all who work to bring aid to the distressed.
Give them wisdom, strength and courage,
and help us to act responsibly in all that we do.
In the name of Jesus Christ our Lord. Amen.

93. Our shared citizenship

We pray, O God, for the peoples of this land:
for those we know and meet,
for people we see or read about in the news,
for people we hear but never encounter,
for people we neither see nor hear
who work behind the scenes to keep the country running,
for the unheralded and untrumpeted,
for the disempowered and needy.
Whatever our race, ethnicity or faith, teach us, O God,
   to grow in our respect for one another as, together,
   we share the life of this nation. Amen.

94. Difficult decisions in society

Where the legitimate needs of individuals in distress
come into conflict with the legitimate concerns of wider societies,
give wisdom to all concerned,
and deliver us from knee-jerk reactions, stiff ideologies
   or inappropriate special pleading.
We pray for refugees and people
who set or enforce immigration policies,
for people needing expensive medical treatment
and for the wider needs of all NHS patients,
for people acting for their family's wellbeing
where this impacts on the wellbeing of wider communities.
In all these complex situations,
help us as a society to find balances
and make decisions that secure the best for all involved,
to provide adequate support for people who suffer
and to safeguard the most vulnerable in our midst.
We pray this in the name of Jesus Christ. Amen.

95. Needs and wants

O holy God,
in a consumer world that seeks to turn our wants into needs,
turn our needs into wants and yearnings
for all that reveals your love and your life
amidst the grasping of our lonely world.
Through Jesus Christ our Lord. Amen.

96. Praying with the news

Help us, our Lord,
to pray for those we do not know and cannot name
who stare at us from our screens and newspapers,
who catch our attention through their eyes
and leave us floundering to know how to respond
to the horrors of their lives.
Grasp and ground our powerless emotion
to turn it into active compassion,
O holy God, we pray. Amen.

Local community life

97. Community life

Lord Jesus, you lived in a local community
and knew its gifts, demands, sorrows and joys:
for our local communities, we give you thanks,
for the neighbours we see on our streets,
for the laughter of children and the pleasure of pets,
the wave from the window and the call to friends.
For the people who provide the local services we rely on:
the street sweepers and refuse collectors,
the police and emergency services,
the people providing buses and taxis, shops and libraries,
and everyone who plays their part to keep community life going.
Bless us all and make us good neighbours to one another,
so that, together, we can build communities of neighbourliness.
In your name we pray, Amen.

98. Community life

Teach us, O Lord, to live together in peace.
Expand our concept of community,
and make us eager to build it locally, nationally and internationally,
bless us with the delight of discovering new neighbours and friends
where we expect to find strangers and enemies,
and challenge us with the demands and rewards
of living as peacemakers wherever we are.
We pray this in the name of the Prince of Peace. Amen.

99. Accessibility issues

We pray for people who find it hard to move around
    in our towns and cities
because of disabilities that make mobility difficult,
and those who encounter unnecessary obstacles in their path
or fear that prevents them from venturing out at all.
Inspire all who design our urban environments
    with creative and accessible solutions to design issues,
and make us all more aware of the way our behaviour
    can help or hinder other people's access,
so that together we create a more considerate society
    that enables all to move about freely.
We pray in the name of Jesus Christ. Amen.

100. Youth and community leaders

Guide and inspire, O Lord,
the work of youth and community leaders
as they seek the wellbeing of young people in situations
where opportunities are few,
resources hard to access,
living conditions unsatisfactory,
and the needs relentless.
We pray for the leaders of church and secular youth groups,
sports teams and clubs for young people,
after-school activities and uniformed organizations.
Give them the vision, enthusiasm and stamina they need
to continue to make a difference for good
in the lives of vulnerable young people.
We pray in the name of Jesus Christ our Lord. Amen.

101. Road safety

Keep us safe on the roads, we pray, O Lord.
Give us the skill and patience
to be careful drivers and cyclists,
and sensible pedestrians.
Alert us when we are tempted to take risks
with our own or other people's lives,
and make us considerate of the needs of all road users.
Keep in safety all who work on the roads:
the police in their traffic duties,
people who drive for a living,
or who repair and maintain the highways and pavements for our benefit.
We pray this in the name of Jesus Christ. Amen.

102. Street life

We pray, Lord Jesus, for people
who work, walk or live on the streets.
Where streets are places of joy and companionship, festival and market,
gladden people's hearts and lives,
but where streets are places of fear, danger or loneliness,
walk alongside those who feel vulnerable or unsafe,
and provide protection for those at risk,
friendship and support for those who have nowhere to turn.
Make us, as a nation, wiser and more attentive
to the needs of everyone who walks the streets of our land.
We pray in the name of our Lord Jesus Christ,
who once walked city streets
and knew both their attraction and their danger. Amen.

103. Unsung people

Thank you, O gracious God,
for the unsung heroes and heroines of daily life.
We pray for people whose faithful work
    and volunteering goes unremarked,
and for the people whose unseen routine actions
enable our daily lives to continue.
We thank you for those who forego food or rest
when they put other people's needs before their own,
or who brave bad weather to restore public services after disruption.
Open our eyes to our dependence upon them;
forgive us when we take their work for granted;
and challenge us to emulate their unheralded service.
We pray this in the name of Jesus Christ. Amen.

DAILY LIFE

Living faithfully

104. Faithful pilgrims

God our Father,
you are ever leading us forward
and calling us to follow you
as faithful and adventurous pilgrims:
give us the courage and the daring
to follow where you lead
and to trust you when the path is not clear,
so that we may be surprised by joy
when we meet you in the unforeseen place,
and strengthened in our faith
when we recognize you in the unexpected guise.
Through Jesus Christ our Lord. Amen.

105. Faithful living

Sweep us up, O Lord,
into the wonder of living faithful lives,
delighting in you and in the people who cross our paths.
Astonish us afresh
with the beauty of your presence and action in our world.
Reframe our limited vision
with the expansiveness of your gracious ways,
and send us as messengers of sheer joy
to a troubled and hurting world.
We pray this in the name of Jesus Christ our Lord. Amen.

106. Ordinary living

O Lord Jesus Christ,
you knew the routines of everyday life
and the necessity to keep going through its ups and downs.
Give us steadiness in our daily living,
especially when it is fraught or demanding.
Deepen our delight in our duties,
expand our relish for doing ordinary things well,
and open our eyes to notice your presence
in the familiar and the mundane.
We pray this in your name. Amen.

107. Undramatic living

Lord, as we pray for people in great need
or facing dramatic circumstances,
we pray too for people who are living ordinary lives,
doing undramatic things with steady purpose and rhythm
    to keep normal life going.
Teach us to value the people who never make headlines
but keep the world ticking over.
Thank you for their prosaic living amidst the familiar hubbub of life.
Help us to live fully and utterly in the present moment
to your glory and for the good of our neighbours. Amen.

108. Ordinary time

Surprise us, Lord God,
with glimpses of your presence amidst the commonplace things of life.
Give us joy
in celebrating the ordinary goodness of the people we meet,
the gift of routine and commitments,
and the potential of unremarkable moments and events
to blossom into something more than we can imagine.
In the name of Jesus Christ our Lord. Amen.

109. Contentment

Teach us, O Lord, to be content with what is life-giving.
Deliver us from hankering after the dazzling and the grandiose
    that leave us discontented and craving for more,
or the frustration of unrealistic expectations.
Help us instead to enjoy the plain and simple wonders around us,
to utilize well the resources we have,
and to take time to appreciate the beauty of wild flowers,
    children's art work, people's smiles and shafts of sunlight.
Give us the priceless gift of contentment with what is attainable
and help us to find satisfaction in having enough.
We pray this in your name. Amen.

110. Following God in daily life

O Lord our God, lead us to follow you day by day.
Guide our feet as we walk in faith and use our hands in your service.
Open our ears to hear the cry of the oppressed.
Open our eyes to notice where there is good that we can do
    and enlarge our hearts to love as you have loved us.
We pray this in the name of Jesus Christ our Lord. Amen.

111. Exploring in life

Make us explorers, O Lord,
drawn by your love,
hearing your voice
 and being open to taking new paths,
so that our journeys may be fruitful.
Spare us from the impatient desire
to see something novel just once,
and help us instead to recognize what we already know
in a different context and in a more illuminating light.
We pray in the name of Jesus Christ. Amen.

112. Silence

Lead us, O Lord,
into a deeper appreciation of silence
and a richer experience of its strange gifts and its many moods.
We pray for people for whom silence is a frightening void that must be filled,
and people for whom silence is impossible
because of the perpetual noise of their surroundings.
Lead us all, O Lord, into the silence of your presence
and teach us to be still and know that you are God. Amen.

113. Living with God's silence

When you test us, O Lord,
with your silence
and ask us to live amidst it,
make our hearing more acute,
our seeing more perceptive,
our trusting more intentional,
and our joy more mature.
In the name of Jesus Christ we pray. Amen.

114. Sitting down*

When we are over-busy,
remind us to sit down,
draw breath
and be attentive to what is happening around us.
Lord Jesus,
you were very busy at times,
so you know the value of time to sit.
We pray for people who have time and space to sit,
for people who feel so pressured they dare not stop and sit,
or who are so weary that they fear they will not be able to get up again.
Help us all to make space to sit and come and sit beside us.
We pray this in your name. Amen.

---

*   Moongalba is the Aboriginal word for a sitting down place

115. Seeing life with God's eyes

Help us, O Lord to look at life through your eyes,
to listen to you in all the noise we hear,
and to turn our lives into prayer that expresses your careful seeing,
acute hearing and compassionate loving. Amen.

116. Transformed living

God our Father,
who, in Jesus Christ, entered our world like a guest gate-crashing a party,
come to us afresh amidst the muddle of our world's life.
Give us the courage to transform our way of living,
and to be heralds of your kingdom coming on earth as it is in heaven.
We pray this in the name of your Incarnate Son,
Jesus Christ our Lord. Amen.

117. The duties of life

Teach us, O Lord, to be faithful in fulfilling the duties of our lives,
and in doing so, keep us open to the
    unexpected in-breaking of new insight and new calling.
We pray in the name of Jesus Christ our Lord. Amen.

118. In times of fear

Astound us, Lord Jesus,
as you did your frightened disciples on the stormy lake.
When the wind is wild,
climb into our boats and still our storms,
then give us a glimpse of your glory.
We pray this not only for ourselves when we are fearful,
but for all people who, even as we pray,
do not know where to turn in their terror.
In your name, O Lord. Amen.

119. God's presence in our lives

Lord, sometimes it feels that you batter our heart,

while at other times you knock almost imperceptibly on our heart's door.

However you come to us,

may we be always open to you,

alert to your gentle pressure upon our lives,

ready to walk steadily in the sunlight you shed upon our path.

Through Christ our Lord. Amen.

120. The gifts and demands of life

Teach us, O God, how to appreciate the gifts of life,

to enjoy the pleasures it offers,

and to savour the memories we build up.

Help us to face the demands of life,

to cope with the difficulties,

and to surprise ourselves

with the resources we discover and draw on.

Guide us, O God,

in the paths of life

and make us good companions

for the people we meet as we live day by day.

We pray in the name of Jesus Christ our Lord. Amen.

121. Focus in our busyness

Amidst the clatter and clutter of daily life,

turn our gaze, O God, to you.

Still our hearts,

silence the noise of our buzzing minds,

and teach us to live more simply,

so that, like Mary, we can choose and live the better part.

We pray in the name of Jesus, our Lord. Amen.

122. When life is confusing
Holy God, to you we turn in the trials and tears of life.
When our doubts and fears conceal your face,
and our cries deafen us to your word of life,
come to us in our confusion
and still us to hear your still small voice
after the earthquake, wind and fire.
Speak our names and lead us as we offer our lives afresh to you.
In the name of Jesus Christ our Lord. Amen.

123. Contradictions and uncertainties in life
Lord Jesus Christ, whose disciples met you in the midst of the storm,
when we face intractable contradictions
     that will not transform into simple resolutions,
give us the courage to live with the grief and the questions,
and to resist the temptation to measure your presence
     by whether or not our lives feel in harmony.
Teach us to live amidst the paradox,
to trust you amidst the uncertainties,
to stay in the place of disturbance,
and to remain with faith in what feels like a gaping void
     between experience and the assurance of your presence.
We pray this in your name, O gracious Saviour. Amen.

124. Unfamiliar territory*
When the frontiers of the familiar suddenly close to us,
when we feel abandoned in an unknown world,
remind us that we have no resting place except in you,
and that we may be called to walk on a road without knowing
where it goes,
O Lord Jesus Christ, our Saviour and our guide. Amen.

---

*   Inspired by words of Dag Hammarskjöld

125. Wilderness living

Teach us, Lord, that nothing is wasted in our lives
and that there is no wasteland that is beyond your presence,
however much it feels like that at times.
We ask this in the name of our Lord Jesus Christ,
who endured the loneliness of the wilderness
    and the abandonment of his friends. Amen.

126. Desert dryness

O holy God, who brought water out of the rock
    for your people in the wilderness,
quench our thirst when we feel parched.
But, further than that, O Lord, remind us
that it is as we share from our dry and rock-like places
    that others will be revived and given life.
Help us, Lord, to believe that our hard places
can be the source of springs of living water for others.
We ask this for your glory's sake, Amen.

127. Reflecting God's glory

O holy God, who spoke and there was light,
shine your holy light on us
and make us prisms of your glory,
refracting your holiness in bright and subtle hues
amidst our world today.
Then stun us into silent wonder
as our lives, with all creation, shout your glory.
Paint our lives with colour, O artist God, we pray. Amen.

128. The goodness of God's love

How good is your love, O God!
Free us from all that holds us back
    from revelling in its depth and savouring its wonder.
Then send us, with hearts filled with love's joy and compassion,
to love a loveless world.
Keep us, O Father, Son and Holy Spirit,
in the love that through your grace we have touched and known. Amen.

129. Memories

Lord, when our long memories serve us well,
strengthen our resolve to live in the light of all that is good in them.
But when our long memories serve only to stoke fear and hatred
    which we cannot explain but feel deep in our being,
then free us from them, heal us and restore our awareness
    of the transformation your new life brings.
We pray this for ourselves and our families,
and for the nations and peoples of the world.
Establish among us all your kingdom of peace.
We pray in the name of Jesus Christ, the Prince of Peace. Amen.

130. Memories

Lord Jesus, at the barbecue on the beach,
you used the smell of a charcoal fire
to remind Peter of his denial and then rework it with him
into a life-changing smell of new beginnings:
we thank you for the sudden, joyful refocusing
when a passing smell runs rampant through our store of memories,
but where those memories are painful or ambivalent
bring your healing, as you did for Peter,
and transform their power to bind into power to love and serve.
This we pray, O risen Lord of barbecues and new beginnings. Amen.

131. Remembering past difficulties

As we look back on times of doubt and fear,
of questions shouted wordlessly,
and of uncertainty and confusion,
remind us, O Lord, that you walked with us,
bearing our griefs and carrying our sorrows,
teaching us afresh new harmonies to the song of our lives.
Give us the courage to sing those new songs as part of our remembering.
We pray this, Lord Jesus, not only for ourselves but for all people
who have known your presence in their suffering. Amen.

132. Living well

Where we are mean-spirited,
O Lord, deliver us from beggarly living.
Where we wreak havoc and destruction,
O Lord, deliver us from careless living.
Where we are fatalistic,
O Lord, deliver us from despairing inaction.
Where we are unconnected with other people,
O Lord, send us out together to live well as your disciples.
In the name of Jesus Christ. Amen.

133. Difficult decisions

When we face difficult decisions, give us, Lord, we pray,
the patience not to act hastily,
the wisdom to discern a prudent course of action,
and the courage to step out in faith and trust.
We pray for all people who will be affected by our decisions,
especially those who will not understand
why that decision has been made.
Make us, O Lord, wise and faithful in the difficult moments of our lives.
We pray in the name of Jesus Christ, Amen.

134. Sharing our gifts

When we are diffident about sharing our gifts and skills with others,
remind us, Lord God,
of the blessing that we have received
when other people have dared to share their gifts for the common good.
We thank you for gifting musicians, artists, poets and authors;
for skills in sports, science, languages and working with our hands;
for inventors and engineers, researchers and surgeons.
Remind us afresh, O Lord,
of our interdependence on one another.
Help us to hone the gifts that you have given each of us,
and give us the blend of courage and reticence
to share them wisely for the good of all.
We pray this in the name of Jesus Christ our Lord. Amen.

135. Overconfidence

When we are overconfident that we are right,
cocooned in the certainty that makes us resistant
to the poetry of wonder and astonishment,
unsettle us, Lord God, with your demanding grace.
Introduce us to the paradoxical gift of precariousness,
and guide us to reach out with reverence to explore and probe
    the mystery of your love.
We pray in the name of Jesus Christ. Amen.

136. Tensions

Help us, O Lord, to deal well with tensions in our relationships,
to pray for each other when we find it hard to talk things through,
to see the best in each other when we prefer to see the worst,
and to be willing to do the slow, sometimes hard, work of reconciliation.
We pray this, Lord Jesus, knowing that you handled
    tensions within your group of disciples,
and that in your hands what is mediocre
can become not only better but very good.
We entrust our tense relationships into your loving hands. Amen.

137. Joy in life

O joyful God, we praise you for the sheer merriment
that at times breaks into our lives and delights us.
We pray for people for whom being glum is such familiar territory
that they find it hard to laugh.
Sweep us all up into the unalloyed joy of your goodness
    unleashed in our world
and teach us to rejoice with you.
We pray in the name of Jesus Christ our Lord. Amen.

138. Joyful service

Inspire us, Lord God,
with your deep joy as you exult over your world with singing.
May our lives sparkle as we reflect your glory,
when we serve you amidst the pain and suffering of your world.
Shine through us to your glory, O Lord, we pray. Amen.

139. Enjoying God's presence

Like spaniels scenting water and children spotting puddles,
give us a homing instinct for your love,
as you gather us, like chicks under their mother's wing,
and keep us in the mutual enjoyment of your presence among us.
In your name we pray, Lord Jesus, Amen.

140. Enjoying God's world

Lord Jesus, who calmed Martha's distraction,
teach us to enjoy the unexpected enchantments of life.
Forgive us when we are too preoccupied to notice the goodness
    that is shining through a raindrop glistening on a leaf,
the glory of a rainbow,
the melodies of birdsong,
the giggling of a child.
Slow us down when we are too busy to enjoy
the deep laughter of companionable moments,
the wagging of a dog's tail,
or the fragrance of a rose.
Keep us alert to the in-breaking of delight
in the midst of the routine and the familiar.
In your name we pray. Amen.

141. God's love and light

O gracious, holy God,
we thank you for the vastness of your love,
its unwieldiness in our world of boundaries and constraints,
its incessant and relentless probing of our lives,
and the way it sheds light into the hidden corners
    that we have never dared to explore.
Help us, O Lord, to walk day by day in the light of your love,
to deal with the dust that it reveals,
and to be light in your world for others.
In the name of Jesus Christ, the light of the world. Amen.

142. Good news

Sweep us up, O Lord, in the gladness of the news of . . .
Thrill us with the beauty of sheer joy,
dare us to live with zest and unalloyed delight
in the goodness that is revealed in your world,
and give us ears to hear the heavenly melody
 as you rejoice over us with singing.
We pray in the name of Jesus Christ,
who rejoiced in you during his life on earth. Amen.

143. Humour

Thank you, Lord God,
for the great gift of humour and for people who make us laugh,
for the grins, chuckles and giggles
that break unannounced into ordinary routines of life.
Make us people of kind laughter, hopeful smiles
and joyful companionship one with another.
In the name of Jesus Christ our Lord. Amen.

144. Humour

Gracious God,
we thank you for the gift of humour
in a world that so often has reason to be sad.
Bless us with joy and laughter at the wonder of your love for us,
and turn us into people who can make others smile.
As we gather to enjoy ourselves,
we remember people in . . . *and other* troubled places,
where there is so little to laugh about.
We pray too that you will bless them
with hope that brings light to their eyes.
We ask this through Jesus Christ our Lord,
who brought joy to those he met. Amen.

145. Laughter

For making a world in which there is the gift of fun and laughter,
we praise you, O Lord.
Free us to enjoy the merriment of being playful,
to revel in the faintly ridiculous,
and to delight in both amusing and being amused.
We thank you for people who can make us laugh
   in kind and healthy ways.
May our humour never be demeaning of other people
or have an uneasy edge to it,
but always honouring to you,
the creator of mirth and rejoicing.
We pray this in the name of Jesus Christ our Lord,
who often taught with a twinkle in his eye. Amen.

146. Being faithful when we are tempted to give up

When we feel regret,
shine your light on the path to a better way.
When we feel anguish,
touch us in our distress with fingertips of grace.
When we are humiliated,
hold your cross before our eyes and remind us
of the joy that was set before you as you bore such shame for us.
When we are jaded,
refresh us with your living water,
so that we, like Peter, may turn
and find you are still calling us to love and serve you.
In your name, we pray, Lord Jesus. Amen.

147. Service in the face of need

Lord, when we feel speechless in the face of the world's needs,
expand our vision into something greater than words.
Reveal to us a beauty and a hope beyond the reach of common sense,
and teach us a new and heavenly harmony
    to the discordant clamour all around.
Stabilize us in your love,
loose our tongues to sing of your salvation,
and send us out to live and work as instruments of your peace.
We pray this in the name of Jesus Christ our Lord. Amen.

148. Serving God in the world

Lord, you challenge us to serve you in the world
and trace your presence in life's daily round.
You call us friends,
bidding us to live with graceful hope
and the wit and will to grasp your ways,
open to glimpse the wonder of your kingdom's scope.
Enlarge our vision so that we can dare to serve you boldly,
and create a place where love is real and raw,
love can be touched,
and the vibrant grace of your kingdom can be expressed on earth.
We pray this for the sake of Jesus Christ our Lord. Amen.

149. Light in the world

Lord, inspire us to light candles in the darkness
    of this world's suffering and shame.
Like flames reflected in a mirror,
show us how to multiply the flickering light,
so that it can speak in simple starkness of new hope born
    in the night of despair and degradation. Amen.

150. Light in the world

Holy God, your radiant and resplendent light
   shone in the face of Jesus Christ,
shine your light in our lives today,
disturb our complacency and expand our hope,
that we may be faithful to our calling as your disciples
   and live as light in the world.
We pray this in the name of Jesus Christ our Lord. Amen.

151. Learning to love

O Lord, teach us the many ways to love
not just the people we rejoice to love,
but the less lovely and the more demanding.
Love us into loving others with your patience and commitment,
so that the world may taste and see your perfect love
revealed in the midst of its all too often loveless life.
We pray this in the name of your beloved Son, Jesus Christ our Lord.
Amen.

152. Life as service

Lord Jesus, you laid aside your rightful reputation
and brought a new way of living
that is free to lay aside fear and love with mercy and vision.
Help us to follow you where you lead us,
to love, to serve, to lay down our own lives.
As we walk your way of humble, costly service,
enlarge our hearts and fill us with compassion
and the commitment to follow you alone. Amen.

153. Responding to need

Remind us, O Lord, when we feel powerless,
that to love someone is to be alongside them,
not to have all the resources they need or all the answers they seek,
and so help us to offer our steady presence.
Forgive us when we seek the comfort of half-truths
or the convenience of evasion
instead of the demand of searing honesty
    in facing the needs that are before us.
We pray in the name of Jesus Christ,
who touched the lives of those around him. Amen.

154. Prayer—not knowing how to pray

When we don't know how to give voice to our prayers,
remind us, O Holy Spirit,
that you pray within us and with us;
in our muteness,
help us to keep our eyes on the one to whom we pray.
In the name of our Lord Jesus Christ. Amen.

155. The history around us

For ancient landscapes that bear silent testimony
to vast histories which make us who we are,
and for the centuries of lived significance of our surroundings,
we praise you, God of the ages.
Slow us down in our exploration of these testaments
    to your faithfulness and our belonging,
and weave into our lives the tales they have to tell.
In the name of Jesus Christ our Lord. Amen.

156. Hurting each other

When, unwittingly, we cut each other
with the serrated edges of our pain,
come, dear Lord, and embrace us with your love.
Then, like a jigsaw, fit our misshapen lives into a glorious whole.
We pray in the name of Jesus Christ our Lord. Amen.

157. Holidays

Lord Jesus, you shared festival times with your family and friends
    away from your home and daily commitments:
we thank you for the gift of holidays and celebrations,
and pray for people who are enjoying a holiday at the moment.
Refresh and renew them through their time away.
We pray, too, for people who would love to have a holiday but cannot do so
because they cannot afford it,
have family or work commitments,
suffer from sickness or infirmity,
or for any other reason.
Bless them as they stay at home
and give them refreshment in their daily routines.
We pray this in your name. Amen.

Morning, noon and evening

158. Morning

We offer the coming day to you, O Lord,
with thanks for having brought us safely through the night,
and we pray for your guidance and protection as the day unfolds.
We offer the work we have to do,
the people we will meet,
the laughter we will share,
and the tasks that will take determination.
May this day be a day of kindliness and goodwill
for everyone with whom we share it.
For the sake of Jesus Christ our Lord. Amen.

159. Morning—stewardship of creation

As we come late to the celebration of another day
    which the birds have sung since dawn,
we pray your blessing on us and on all your creation
    in its timeless beauty and its daily need.
This day may we be good stewards of your good earth.
In your name we pray. Amen.

160. Morning

When a beautiful day dawns,
we give you thanks for the wonders around us.
When a cold, wet day dawns,
we pray for people ill-equipped to meet it.
When a special day dawns,
we pray for people who will celebrate.
When a difficult day dawns,
we pray for people who will be glad when it is over.
However people live today,
may they know your presence and your care surrounding them,
O God, our loving Father. Amen.

161. Morning—Christ, whose glory fills the skies*

"Christ, whose glory fills the skies":
open our eyes today to the glory of your creation.
"Christ, the true, the only light":
flood your world with light in the dark and hidden places
where sin and suffering hide from sight.
"Dark and cheerless is the morn unaccompanied by thee":
lift the gloom that faces many people as they wake today.
"Joyless is the day's return 'till thy mercy's beams I see":
shed your mercy on all who cry out to you today,
and on those whose suffering has silenced them.
In the coming day, Lord Christ, may your glory fill the world. Amen.

162. Morning

At the start of a new day we pray, O Lord,
for ourselves as we prepare for all that it will bring,
for the people we will meet,
that our encounters will be life-giving,
the people who will keep our communities running,
those charged with governance in its many forms,
and people who are in danger of having their needs overlooked.
For each of us, O Lord, we pray for the resources necessary
    for a good and healthy life,
so that by this evening we can say it has been a day well lived. Amen.

163. Morning

O Lord, our God, we join with all creation in singing your praise
for a new day with its new beginnings and challenges,
familiar routines and old responsibilities.
Bless us as we live this day in your sight
and with your strength. Amen.

---

* From a hymn by Charles Wesley

164. Morning

At the beginning of this new day, we offer you, O Lord,
our anticipation of all that lies ahead:
the prospects that fill us with joy,
and those that we face with apprehension.
Guide our footsteps as we live this day with you.
Amen.

165. Morning—for those facing difficulties

O holy God, as this new day begins,
we pray for people for whom it will be difficult,
may bring bad news or place them in danger.
Shield them from harm
and provide the support and care they need.
In the name of Jesus Christ our Lord. Amen.

166. Morning

As we stand, O God, on the cusp of a new day,
open our eyes to your presence in the world around us,
stun us with glimpses of beauty,
use us to be your channels of grace,
stir us to appropriate thoughts and actions,
and shield us from harm.
For the sake of Jesus Christ our Lord. Amen.

167. Midday

Lord, as we pause in the middle of the day,
help us to be aware of your presence with us.
We remember the people we have met this morning,
the tasks we have done,
the work in progress,
and the problems still to be solved.
We pray for your guidance in all that lies before us this afternoon.
Lead us, O Lord, in your paths of righteousness.
We pray this in the name of Jesus Christ our Lord. Amen.

168. Midday—people in their work

We pray, O Lord, for people who today will have
    an impact on the lives of others:
for politicians in national and local government
and staff who administer their decisions,
for bankers, market traders, and all who influence the financial markets,
for all who keep our communities running:
the police and emergency services,
teachers, medical staff and care workers,
people working in retail, transport, leisure and cultural sectors,
for social services and the ministry of communities of faith,
and for good neighbours everywhere.
Enable us today to work together for the good of all.
We pray in your name, Lord Jesus. Amen.

169. Midday—suffering in the world

Heal gently, O Lord, the people for whom this morning
    has brought illness, injury, sorrow or distress;
and bless the people who are working to restore
    order and peace in their lives.
Be present, this noon, O Lord, in places of suffering and healing.
In your name we pray. Amen.

170. Evening

This evening, turn our hearts and minds to you, O God,
as we offer you the day that is passing:
We give thanks for all that has brought us joy and life,
hold in your presence all that has troubled or distressed us,
and we pray for your wisdom in all that still perplexes or stretches us.
As evening falls, grant us your peace, we pray. Amen.

171. Evening—unfinished work

We bring our unfinished work this evening, O Lord,
and ask for the grace to commit it to you in trust.
We bring our memories of all we have achieved today,
asking you to prosper all that is good and restrain all that is amiss.
We bring the people we have met today
(whom we name in silence . . .)
and pray your blessing on them this evening.
At the end of the day, may your presence go with us
and give us peace. Amen.

172. Evening—people who have suffered

As we look back on the day that is passing,
we pray, O God, not just for our own concerns
but for the needs of your wider world.
We pray for people whose lives have been turned upside down today
by joy or sorrow, accident or disaster,
and ask your peace and healing for those who suffer
    this evening because of events today.
We pray, too, for people who even now are working
    to bring relief to people in need,
and those who will work through the night on behalf of others.
In the name of Jesus Christ our Lord. Amen.

173. Evening—people who work through the night

As we prepare to rest, O Lord, we pray for people
    who will work through the night:
for nurses, doctors and care workers,
for the emergency services,
and people who keep public transport and factories running,
for the people who clean buildings
    and sweep streets while they are empty,
for members of religious communities
    who will wake in the darkness to pray,
and for parents and carers who will be woken from sleep
    to tend to the needs of others.
May they each know your presence with them in the hours of darkness,
Lord Jesus, the light of the world. Amen.

174. Evening—people who work through the night

We pray for people who will work through the coming night
so that we can sleep in safety and in peace.
May those in the emergency or medical and caring services,
in industry or offices,
or in transport or service industries
know your presence and protection in their work and in their travel.
Prosper their work for the good of all people.
We pray this in the name of Jesus Christ our Lord. Amen.

175. Evening—sleep

This evening, as we thank you for the gift of sleep,
we pray for people who will not sleep well tonight:
for people whose pain keeps them awake,
and people who fear for their safety if they go to sleep,
for people whose sleep is tormented by nightmares,
and people who have nowhere comfortable to sleep.
We pray, too, for people whose sleep will be broken
   by noise, disturbance or the needs of others.
O Lord, give us all your peace through the coming night,
and may we wake refreshed for the day ahead.
We pray in the name of Jesus Christ,
who, at times, did not sleep through the night. Amen.

176. Evening—sleep

We pray tonight for people for whom sleep will be hard.
For people suffering unremitting pain or sickness,
who are troubled by nightmares,
or whose worries are amplified in the small hours.
For people who feel unsafe in their homes
or who have no shelter but sleep on the streets.
O Lord, grant them the blessing of refreshing sleep
and the strength to face tomorrow. Amen.

177. Evening—rest

Grant us rest tonight, O gracious God:
the rest of refreshment for the exhausted,
the rest of healing for the sick,
the rest of calming for the troubled,
and the rest of peace for the dying.
Awaken us tomorrow with renewed joy
and energy for the day ahead.
In the name of Jesus Christ we pray. Amen.

178. Evening—end of a busy day
Lord, at the end of another day,
when life has at times been dull or over-busy
or when we are tired and crotchety,
refresh us in these moments of prayer,
and tomorrow send us back to our duties with renewed enthusiasm,
and with the expectation that we might meet with you
    in the most mundane of tasks.
We offer all we have done today into your hands. Amen.

Homes and hospitality

179. Hospitality
O God of feast and festival,
of family and home,
of companionship and celebration,
surprise us afresh with your welcome and hospitality.
Inspire us to welcome the people who come to us,
not just the expected but also the unlikely or inconvenient guest.
Lord Jesus, come among us through your people.
In your name we pray. Amen.

180. Welcoming homes

May our homes, O God, be places of welcome and refreshment,
of good company and good conversation,
of joy and laughter, inspiration and ideas.
While we give thanks for happy homes,
we pray for the homes of families under stress,
and homes where there is loneliness or abuse,
domestic violence or neglect.
Lord Jesus, you knew the security and challenges of family life;
bless our homes and families today.
In your name we pray. Amen.

181. Hospitality and new beginnings

Lord Jesus, your answer to your friends' betrayal
    was to cook breakfast for them.
Lift us above motives of retribution or revenge,
and open our hearts to welcome the people who, like your disciples,
    most need a new beginning in their lives.
In your name we pray. Amen.

Work

182. Our daily work

Lord God, at the beginning of the day,
we offer you our work in the coming hours
[at the end of the day, we offer you the work we have done today].
May it be productive and done well,
to prosper the wellbeing of the world in which we serve.
In the name of Jesus Christ,
who worked at a carpenter's bench. Amen.

183. Many kinds of work

Lord God our creator,
we pray for scientists who probe the mysteries of your creation;
for medical researchers who seek ways to harness
    the resources of your world to bring health and healing;
for people working in technology and industry
    who develop new ways to further human wellbeing;
for farmers, gardeners and vets who grow our food and tend animals;
for artists in all media who create new expressions of life and beauty
    to challenge and enliven us;
and for ourselves, that we will use wisely
the skills and interests you have given us.
May your Holy Spirit inspire and enthuse us in our daily work. Amen.

184. People who clean up

Lord, we pray for people who clean up after us,
those who do it for love and those who do it for low wages.
Thank you for their care of our environment.
Bless the people who clean our streets, our schools and our hospitals,
    our public toilets, our shopping centres, and our places of work,
    our homes, our public transport and our polluted rivers,
and those who collect our rubbish and work in recycling centres.
Forgive us when we take them for granted
    and don't acknowledge their presence,
keep them safe from harm if they have to travel at unsocial hours,
protect them from the health hazards they encounter,
give them stamina for their work, adequate rest times
and right recompense for their toil on our behalf,
stir us to follow their example of caring for our shared environment.
In the name of Jesus Christ our Lord. Amen.

185. Hard or demeaning work

Lord Jesus, you knew the demands, frustrations and satisfactions
   of work as a carpenter.
Surround with your protection and love
all people who today work for their living,
especially those who find it hard or demeaning.
Bless all who seek for work in the face of despondency and despair.
In your name we pray. Amen.

186. Work at sea

When we hear the familiar rhythmic litany of
"Fastnet, Irish Sea, Shannon, Rockall, Malin, Hebrides",
remind us, O Lord, to pray for the people
   for whom the shipping forecast may be
   literally a matter of life and death:
for those who work in the fishing industry, especially those in small
   boats, and the people at the harbours who depend on their catch,
for the sailors on container ships, living far from home for months,
for those who run the ferries maintaining contact between islands,
for those on the yachts and pleasure craft enjoying life on the sea,
for the RNLI, the Mission to Seafarers and the Royal Navy in their work.
Lord Jesus, who knew the Sea of Galilee so well,
bless and protect all who sail the seas and oceans today. Amen.

187. Work in bad weather

When the weather is bad, Lord,
we pray you will protect all people who have no option but to be out in it,
the people whose work requires them to be outside,
    undertaking tasks we take for granted so barely notice:
people who keep our streets clean, drive buses and taxis,
deliver goods to homes and businesses,
repair roads and pavements,
those who maintain the emergency services,
for market traders, construction workers,
and those selling the *Big Issue* or waiting for a shelter to open.
As we are grateful for boots and umbrellas,
and homes where we can dry out or warm up,
bless the people who have to get cold and wet.
We pray this in the name of Jesus Christ,
who walked the roads in all weathers. Amen.

188. Unemployment

We pray, O Lord, for all who are unemployed and their families:
for people who have never worked and those who have lost their jobs,
for people without the necessary skills for a job,
or whose health or family circumstances reduce their flexibility
in a competitive market,
for people who find regular commitment difficult,
and those whose skills do not match the opportunities available.
Give them hope in their search for work;
guide them to sources of help and training,
and give patience and creative compassion to people
    who work in job centres and benefits offices.
We pray this in the name of Jesus Christ. Amen.

Education and learning

189. Study

Lord, open our minds and hearts to know you
  through your word and world.
Free us from the confines of our preconceptions
  and unlock our minds to wonder.
Holy Spirit of God, Advocate and Guide,
  open our eyes and hearts to your presence in what we read and study.
Tingle our ears with new perspectives.
Extend the horizon to which we gaze and send us out
renewed and refreshed with a gospel to proclaim. Amen.

190. Study

God our creator, we thank you for the exhilarating
  breadth and depth of human knowledge,
and for the humbling realization that after a lifetime of
  study we have only skirted the edges of your ways.
We pray for all teachers and students in our
  schools, colleges and universities.
Give them inquiring and perceptive minds, skill
  to learn and wisdom to ask significant questions,
so that we may love you with all our mind, and with all our strength.
Further our use of knowledge for the common good.
Make us wise stewards of our learning
and compassionate in its application for the good of your creation.
We ask this in the name of your Son, Jesus Christ our Lord. Amen.

191. Places of study

Gracious God, you are the source of all wisdom
    and the giver of all good gifts.
We pray for all who are involved in the world of education,
for the universities, colleges, schools and Sunday schools
    in this *county / city / town / diocese of . . .* ,
for all who teach, all who study and all who work behind the scenes
    to create the environments in which learning can flourish.
Grant your blessing on our places of study.
May good learning abound and prosper,
may inquisitive minds be nurtured and stretched,
may new knowledge lead people to deeper wisdom,
and may your world be changed for the better as wisdom is applied.
We pray this in the name of Jesus Christ our Lord. Amen.

192. New academic term

At the start of a new *school / university* term,
we pray for all returning students and teachers
and for those who are new and apprehensive.
May this term begin well,
new friendships and communities of learning built,
new insights gained
and new confidence developed.
We pray this in the name of Jesus Christ our Lord. Amen.

193. Struggling at school

We pray for children who struggle at school,
for the lonely and fearful,
the awkward and the troubled,
those with special needs
and all who, for whatever reason, find learning difficult.
Inspire their teachers with the patience and wisdom
    to know how to support them,
and give them friends among their peers,
so that their school days may be times of joy
rather than fear or distress.
We pray in the name of Jesus Christ our Lord. Amen.

194. Struggling to learn

We pray for people who find it hard to learn:
For those with no access to educational opportunities,
for all who are denied such opportunities as exist,
for those with learning difficulties,
who lack the support they need to learn,
for those for whom early struggles to read and write
    have led to ongoing disadvantage,
and for those whose sense of curiosity about the world
    has been silenced by the actions of others.
O God, give wisdom to all people who have responsibility
    for education policy, funding and delivery,
so that all your people around the world may rejoice
in discovering the wonders of your world.
We pray this in the name of Jesus Christ our Lord. Amen.

195. Exams

In this exam season,
we pray for students sitting exams,
teachers marking exams,
and decisions taken from the results of exams.
Grant your peace to all involved
    in these stressful yet vital times of assessment.
We pray in the name of Jesus Christ our Lord. Amen.

Creativity and the arts

196. Creativity

Creator God,
your world is beautified by the arts that unfurl new glimpses of glory
and express the joys and sorrows of our lives.
Make us wise stewards of our own creativity,
that we may use our gifts for the wellbeing of the world you created,
and for the healing of lives that are blighted by ugliness and despair.
We pray this in the name of Jesus Christ our Lord. Amen.

197. Music and / or art

Gracious God, artist and composer of a world full of sight and sound,
accept our praise for the gift of music and art.
Inspire our hearts with the music made here today
    (the artwork seen here today),
and stir our wills to follow you where this music *(art)* leads us.
In the name of Jesus Christ our Lord we pray. Amen.

198. Music

Creator God,
we give you thanks for the gift of music and the skill of musicians.
May our prayer and praise ever reflect
the beauty of the worship in heaven,
where saints and angels sing your praise,
and the creativity of this world,
where you have given us minds and hearts to use to your glory.
May our music-making always bring honour to your name. Amen.

199. Creativity

Creator God, whose world is full of infinite wonders,
we rejoice in the creative impulse you have placed in humanity,
and pray that each person may discover some gift that they can develop
    to give voice and form to what is deep within them.
We pray for children whose creative voice is already stifled;
for adults who are haunted by memories
    of being told their efforts were no good;
and for people who do not have the opportunities
    to develop the gifts that they yearn to express.
Help us to value our own and other people's creativity,
so that, together, we will make our corner of the world
    ever more expressive of your generous goodness.
We pray this in the name of Jesus Christ our Lord. Amen.

200. Art therapy

For the grace and insight of artists who are able to draw art and
    beauty out of trouble and distress, we give you thanks, O God.
As we draw inspiration from their works, we pray for art therapists,
    and for all who seek to help others find freedom
    by giving artistic expression to their pain.
In the name of Jesus Christ our Lord. Amen.

201. Storytelling

We thank you, Lord Jesus, for the wonderful stories you told.
Give us the blessing today of good stories and good storytellers.
Through them, open our hearts and minds to new possibilities
and new ideas that lead us into creative ways of faithful living.
Inspire authors and publishers, actors and broadcasters,
    parents and teachers,
in the creation and telling of good stories,
and give us the delight of children in hearing them.
We pray this in your name. Amen.

FAMILIES AND FRIENDS

Relationships

202. Family and friends

We pray for our families and friends,
for those whose love has nurtured and sustained us,
given us courage to follow our dreams,
and warned us of pitfalls or when we overstretch ourselves;
we pray for people whose absence
would make our lives easier but poorer;
help us to appreciate them in deeper ways.
We pray for families under stress,
for families where love is rationed and words are barbed,
for families facing unemployment, benefit delays or financial strain,
    sickness or special need, violence or abuse, sorrow or bereavement,
and for people who are lonely,
whether they are on their own or surrounded by others.
We pray for all who work in whatever way to support family life.
Help us to be good homemakers, Lord, we pray. Amen.

203. Family and friends

Gracious God, we pray for our families and our friends.
Strengthen and protect them day by day,
and give them wisdom in the round of daily life.
Bless our children as they grow up and keep them safe from harm.
Give wisdom to those we love when they face difficulties,
and your strength to members of our families
    who are ill or face troubles.
Help us to entrust them to your loving care,
and give us your peace in this time of separation from them.
We ask this in the name of Jesus Christ our Lord. Amen.

204. Family and friends

Lord Jesus, you knew the delight and the demands
    of life in a family or with close friends,
and you knew that companionship is both discipline and gift:
We pray for the needs of our own families and circle of friends
    (especially those we name in silence),
    giving thanks for all they share with us, and praying for their needs;
may our presence in their lives be a source of blessing day by day.
In your name we pray. Amen.

205. Friendship

For the gift of friendship, we give you thanks, O God,
and we pray for the people we are privileged to call our friends.
May we, in turn, be good friends to them
and to others we meet in daily life.
Strengthen the bonds of companionship
and enable us to offer mutual support, delight and challenge.
We pray this in the name of Jesus Christ our Lord. Amen.

206. Friendship

Lord Jesus Christ, you chose people to be your friends from all walks of life,
with different personalities and shades of opinion.
As we read of your times spent with friends,
teach us afresh of the joys and demands of true friendship,
so that we may be willing, as you were, to take the risk
of extending friendship to unlikely and unexpected people,
as well as to those who share our interests and backgrounds.
Lord Jesus, build your Church as a place where
    friendships are true and reliable,
so that, together as friends,
we may reach out to a world in need.
In your name we pray. Amen.

207. Friendship

Give us, dear Lord,
the stamina to sustain deep friendships
that enable us to face the hard times together,
the honesty to know and be known by those we call close friends,
the openness to welcome new friends when our paths cross in new ways,
and the joy in other people that makes us a delight to be with,
    whether for an hour or for a lifetime.
We pray this in your name, Lord Jesus Christ,
friend to so many during your life on earth. Amen.

208. Joy and refreshment

Lord Jesus, help us to imagine the evenings you spent with your friends
after the rigorous days of travel and crowds:
the preparation and sharing of meals,
the telling of jokes and stories,
the singing of familiar songs,
the seeing of familiar faces through the flicker of oil lamps or open fires,
the camaraderie and the commitment.
May our lives be similarly punctuated
by outbursts of joy and refreshment.
Bless us, our families, friends and colleagues.
In your name we pray. Amen.

209. Family and community centres

We thank you, Lord Jesus, for the companionship
that you shared with your disciples and wider circle of friends,
and for the companionship we share
with our family and friends, for whom we pray.
We pray, too, for people who find it hard to meet with others,
and for the work of local community centres
    and clubs for the elderly and lonely.
May they share the joy you knew with your companions.
We pray this in your name, Amen.

210. People who are distant from us

Heavenly Father, we pray for people we love but who are distant from us.
For the gift of friendship and companionship we give you thanks,
and we pray that you will strengthen the ties between us,
    despite the separation of distance or circumstance.
In the name of Jesus Christ our Lord. Amen.

211. Mothering / Mothering Sunday

Lord Jesus Christ, you knew the joy of having a loving, faithful mother.
We give you thanks for all mothers
and people called to a mothering role.
We pray for them, especially for people who find the demands on them
    stretch them to the limits of their resources.
We pray for people who have had no example of
    being well-nurtured by a mother,
whose memories of their mother are sad, fearful or non-existent,
and ask that (*on this Mothering Sunday)* you will gather them,
    like a mother hen gathering her chicks,
        into the safety of your kind embrace.
In your name we pray. Amen.

212. Remembering the dead

O heavenly Father, as we remember our loved ones and friends
who have died *in the last year / from cancer / in accidents / violent deaths . . .* ,
we entrust them to your merciful care,
and we pray for the peace and assurance of your love for them and us.
Help us to grieve with sorrow at our loss
    and with joy at our memories of their life among us.
Where those memories are ambivalent or painful,
free us from their grip and sting.
We pray in the name of Jesus Christ our Lord,
who wept at the tomb of his friend Lazarus. Amen.

People and families under stress or with special needs

213. Financial pressures

Lord Jesus, you entrusted the common purse to Judas who stole from it
and so know how sensitive decisions over shared finance can be:
We pray for families where money divides people one from another,
for families where hard decisions must be made
because there is not enough money for basic living, disagreement
    about priorities, or bitterness over unrealistic expectations.
We pray, too, for households where one person
    squanders the resources meant for all,
and families where there is acrimony
over inheritance or divorce settlements.
In all such situations, we pray for the establishment of trusting
    relationships, access to appropriate advice and support,
        and ways forward for the good of all, especially those most vulnerable.
In your name we pray. Amen.

214. Families with special needs

Lord Jesus, you lived in a family, sharing its delights and demands:
We pray for families where life is controlled by the special needs of one
    member that are hard to balance with the needs of everyone else.
We pray for siblings who feel overlooked by their parents,
for teenagers who resent the presence of a demanding grandparent,
for children who must care for a parent
while keeping their schoolwork and social life in balance,
for parents who feel their own relationship is threatened
    by the constant demands of a child with special needs,
and for all who are simply exhausted.
For all these people, we pray for an infusion of your loving care
and strength mediated in unexpected, gifted ways.
In your name. Amen.

215. Widowed people

Send your blessing, O God,
on people who find it hard to adjust to having lost their partners.
We pray for people whose loneliness gnaws at their wellbeing,
those daunted by the administration after a death
or whose housing is unsuitable for their future.
We pray for elderly or physically challenged people
    who cannot take on the roles their partner fulfilled
and do not have family or friends on hand to help.
We pray for people whose grief overwhelms them,
and for people for whom the death of a partner
    is a relief they dare not name in public.
As your Son ensured that his widowed mother
    was cared for by your disciple John,
so we pray for an increase in good neighbourliness,
practical kindness and compassion.
In the name of Jesus Christ. Amen.

216. Marriages under pressure

We pray, O loving Lord, for marriages and partnerships
    that are under pressure.
Bless couples who struggle to develop or maintain
    a loving, healthy relationship,
whose dreams lie shattered
and who cause each other pain rather than joy.
Guide them to the support and resources that can help them through
    the troubled times towards a renewed and life-giving relationship,
protect their children from the scars of distressed family life,
and give them the courage to secure a place of safety
    for anyone affected by domestic violence.
O Lord Jesus, help us all to build loving and safe relationships
    that reflect your love for us.
In your name we pray. Amen.

217. Broken families

We pray, O Lord, for families that face break-up or have broken up.
For adults and children scarred
by the heartbreak and anger of divorce or separation,
that they might find help to find new and healthy ways of relating
after the breakdown,
for family members who have been taken to a place of safety,
that they might find help to rebuild their lives in new and safe ways,
for families in which someone has disappeared
without explanation or trace,
that they might find your comfort and sustenance
amidst the aching void and unanswered questions.
Prosper, we pray, the work of statutory and voluntary
     agencies which support good family life,
and strengthen family members who have to pick up the pieces
amidst their own mixed emotions.
We pray this, Lord Jesus, in your dear name. Amen.

218. Parents under pressure

Lord Jesus Christ, we pray for parents under extreme pressure,
who do their best to raise children in harsh circumstances
     caused by poverty, ill-health, addiction, domestic violence
     or any other life-diminishing circumstances.
We pray for their children living in these situations,
asking that you will lead them to the support and resources
     that can lift some of their burdens.
Hear us as we pray for all people involved in the provision
of statutory or charitable services to support and enhance family life.
We pray in your name, O Lord. Amen.

219. Missing people

We pray, O Lord, for people who have gone missing
   from their homes and communities,
for those who have been abducted,
and for those who have disappeared for their own reasons, *especially for . . .*
We pray for their safety, wellbeing and protection from malice and harm.
We pray, too, for their families and friends,
   that you will provide comfort and hope
   in the midst of fear and despair.
Prosper the work of everyone who searches for missing people.
We ask this in the name of Jesus Christ our Lord,
who was himself missing for three days as a child. Amen.

220. Strained relationships

Lord Jesus, you knew times of strained relationships
with your disciples or people you met, especially religious leaders.
When we read of families in the Bible which faced tension or dissension,
we are reminded that there have always been
   tensions in close relationships.
We pray for members of our family, social or work circles
   with whom we find it hard to get along.
Show us, Lord, how to find ways to make life less tense or argumentative.
Help us to be aware of what is, or could be, good in each relationship,
and to appreciate the not-always-welcome gifts that we offer each other.
We pray this in your name, Lord Jesus. Amen.

Children

221. Children

Lord Jesus Christ,
you were a friend of children when you lived on earth.
Thank you for all children we know,
particularly those in our families and local schools.
We pray, too, for children across the world,
especially those whose lives are insecure:
children who are orphaned, homeless, abused, frightened or sick,
and all who do not have the care and support we take for granted.
Please bless them today,
and show us ways to help and support them.
We ask this in your name. Amen.

222. Children's development

Lord Jesus Christ, you once saw the world with the wonder of a child
and asked the impossible questions of childhood.
We give you thanks for the blessing and the responsibility of children,
our own or those we meet in our daily life.
We pray for them at school, at home and at play,
for their security and protection from harm
and for their growth and development in knowledge and understanding.
Bless all parents, foster parents and all who work with children,
and give us childlike delight in the good things of your world.
We pray this in your name, Amen.

223. Children who are unsafe

We pray for children who feel unsafe in their own homes,
may they find places of safety;
we pray for children who have no homes or live in inadequate homes,
may they find a place to call their own;
we pray for children who care for their parents in their homes,
may they find the support services they need;
we pray for children who have had to leave their parents' homes,
may they find good foster or adoptive homes;
and we pray for social workers who specialize in working with children,
may they find fulfilment in their work
and have the support they need to assist the children in their care.
In the name of Jesus Christ our Lord. Amen.

224. Children with special needs

We pray for families with children who have special needs:
for children with chronic illness, physical disabilities
or developmental needs,
children needing special educational provision
    or whose particular needs disrupt family life,
and for children whose need for specialist care
    separates them from their families.
We pray for parents and foster parents,
for siblings and extended families.
Bless these children and their families
and provide them with all that is best
    for their healthy growth and development.
We pray this in the name of Jesus Christ our Lord. Amen.

225. Children's delight

Teach us, through children, to rediscover our delight
   in your world and in its exploration,
to value friendships and care for those we love,
to play freely and laugh gladly,
to turn unashamedly for help when we need it,
and to focus intently when something catches our attention.
Lord Jesus, we remember how you took a child and sat it on your knee:
love and care for the children we know or see in our neighbourhood
and make them a blessing to others. Amen.

226. Adoption and fostering

We pray for children and young people
who are waiting for fostering or adoption,
and for those who are settling into new families.
Bless the work of adoption agencies and council fostering services,
and all families who welcome children who are not their own.
Give them joy in their expanded family life,
resilience in the difficult times,
and healing of past pain or trauma.
We pray, too, for parents who have had to give up
   their children for fostering or adoption,
and ask that they find the help they need in life.
In your name we pray, Lord Jesus Christ. Amen.

Older people

227. Older people

O God of Abraham, your call still comes to us,
our age is no barrier to your mighty ways.
May we, like Abraham in his old age,
be alert to your call and your companionship.
We pray for older people, giving thanks for their presence among us.
Bless them with your peace and assurance
    of your presence in the lonely times,
provide people to support them in their needs,
and give them clarity and joy in their memories.
In the name of Jesus Christ our Lord. Amen.

228. God's faithfulness through life

O faithful God,
your love is new each day
and has proven strong and true through the years.
As we look back on the past, with both gratitude and regret,
we turn to you, O steadfast God,
in our weakness and our strength.
Grant us the grace ever to turn to you in daily life,
to keep an open heart ready to prove your faithfulness,
and to walk with you in faith through life's remaining days.
We pray this in the name of Jesus Christ our Lord. Amen.

229. Older people who need care

Lord Jesus, who entrusted your mother to the care of your friend,
we pray for the older people we know:
for those able to care for themselves,
those who live in care homes and nursing homes,
and for those struggling with dementia.
Give patience and wisdom to them, their families and carers.
We pray, too, for older people who are left to cope on their own
without the resources they need for a dignified standard of life.
Keep us alert to the needs of older people we meet,
so we can care for them well,
helping them to live life to the fullest and with dignity.
In your name we pray. Amen.

230. The restrictions of old age

We pray, dear Lord, for older people whose minds
   are still active but whose bodies are not.
May they find the support they need
as they face the frustrations and limitations of restricted living
which make ordinary tasks so cumbersome and time-consuming.
Give them joy in the stimulation of absorbing mental activity
and contact with people who share their interests.
Guide us in our contact with older people
to know how best to support them in their endeavours.
We pray in the name of Jesus Christ. Amen.

231. Older Christians

We praise you, Lord God, for the faithfulness
of Elizabeth and Zechariah, Simeon and Anna,
the elderly people who played their unanticipated parts
   in the incarnation of your Son.
Bless their counterparts today in their age-long fidelity,
and give us the wisdom to ask them to teach us
to sing your song of praise today. Amen.

232. Age and infirmity

When age or infirmity makes us crotchety,
forgive us, O God,
and restore our equanimity by reminding us
   of the many blessings of life.
If we are ill or in need of help,
enable us to bear our situation with grace rather than cantankerousness,
and show us the funny side of life,
so that we can laugh with, rather than moan at,
   the people who offer to help us.
As we pray this for ourselves, now or in the future,
we pray for people who are already finding it hard
   to be old or infirm with goodwill,
and we ask that you will comfort and encourage them
   with hope for the days ahead.
In the name of Jesus Christ, we pray. Amen.

233. Grandparents

We pray for grandparents who, for whatever reason,
   find themselves raising their grandchildren,
and who, being older, feel themselves stretched
by the needs and energy of young people
on whom they cannot shut the door—as other grandparents can—
at the end of a visit.
Give them wisdom, stamina and imagination
to forge new bonds across the generations.
Strengthen their family life and give them joy
while they fulfil this role in the lives of their grandchildren.
We pray in the name of Jesus Christ, Amen.

234. Older people and children

We praise you, O Lord,
for grandparents, great-aunts and great-uncles:
for the love they can offer to children,
for the time to enjoy activities together across the generations,
and the insights and wisdom that come from life-experience.
Bless the relationships between children and older people
for the mutual flourishing of both.
We pray in the name of Jesus Christ. Amen.

PEOPLE IN NEED

People in need

235. People who are hurting
God of unfathomable love,
when life is brimming with suffering,
touch with healing gentleness;
when eyes are filled with tears,
wipe with smiling gentleness;
when ears are deafened by screams of hatred,
soothe with a lullaby of gentleness;
when hearts are broken by cruelty,
fill the numbed void with gentle love.
And show us how we can be ministers of your grace
to a hurting world. Amen.

236. Isolated people
Make your gentle presence known, Lord Jesus, we pray,
to people who feel isolated or forgotten,
and who yearn in their loneliness
for the presence and touch of someone else.
Whatever the circumstances of their isolation,
may they find comfort and new
hope through a sense of your loving arms
    surrounding and upholding them.
We pray this in your name, O kind and loving Lord. Amen.

237. Loneliness, our response

We pray, dear Lord, for people who are lonely;
for all who are isolated
and for those who are lonely within the crowds around them.
Lord Jesus, you knew the power of touch to affirm and heal,
we offer you the power of touch of our own hands,
to use in your service;
you knew the power of the human voice to reassure
and assuage the fear and isolation,
we offer you our voices,
to speak and sing where words and song are missing from people's lives;
you knew the power of human companionship
in the routine hours and tasks of daily life,
we offer you our bodies,
to be alongside the isolated and unfriended.
As we pray for lonely people,
stir us into gentle, loving and practical responses
to needs that we are able to meet.
We pray this in your name. Amen.

238. Separation

We pray, O Lord, for people who are separated from those they love:
for people in hospitals, hospices or care homes
whose family and friends cannot visit as they would wish,
for families and communities separated
by political regimes and military forces,
for children and parents separated through the need
    to secure the safety and wellbeing of the vulnerable,
for prisoners, refugees, overseas workers
and people who have lost touch with their families.
For all of these people we pray your comfort, Lord,
when the aching of absence becomes intolerable,
and any hope of reunion is shrouded
    by the loneliness of the present moment.
We ask this in your name, Lord Jesus,
recalling your cry of anguish when you were separated from your Father,
knowing you understand people's sorrow. Amen.

239. Restricted lives

Lord Jesus Christ, you came to share our life,
so that we might have abundant life,
yet you wept in times of sorrow.
We pray for people whose lives feel constrained or constricted,
who are more familiar with tears than joy,
or who have faced sudden sorrow that diminishes their joy.
Teach us how to weep with those who weep (*especially . . .*)
and to offer them our presence alongside them or in prayer,
until the night of weeping is over and joy comes with the morning.
Then bring them compassionate people
who will gently wipe the tears from grieving eyes
and assure them of your presence in the days ahead.
We pray this in your name, kind Lord. Amen.

240. Intense suffering

When suffering feels fathomless,
stabilize us with the benchmark of your compassion
and stir us back to action;
when consolation seems impossible,
fill broken hearts with your succour
and make us instruments of your peace;
when the cry of anguish echoes around the world
but goes unheeded in the corridors of power,
shake up our shared complacency
and set in motion a daring response of love.
In your name we pray, O Lord, Amen.

241. Intense suffering

In the face of strident howls of anguish,
strengthen the hope that dares to shout so that others will hear.
In the face of despair that dulls eyes to silent stares,
strengthen the hope that dares to sparkle, even briefly.
In the face of hunger that gnaws relentlessly,
strengthen the will of others to provide food;
and in the face of the pain that breaks hearts,
strengthen the love that brings healing.
O Lord Jesus, you knew the human condition
and wept in the face of the suffering you encountered.
Steel us to be instruments of your love in a hurting world. Amen.

242. The harshness of life

When we meet people for whom the harshness of living lines their faces,
    scars their hands and is etched into their lives,
stop us from being daunted by their suffering.
Instead, expand our compassion for what they have endured,
and draw out from us and our society constructive responses
    to needs that go untended in our neighbourhoods.
We pray this in the name of Jesus Christ our Lord. Amen.

243. People who seek for God

Lord, we pray for people everywhere
who feel that searching for you is like entering a maze
with no way forward and no way back.
Turn the maze into a labyrinth,
give them joy in the adventure it offers,
lead them to the centre and to your heart of love. Amen.

244. Looking for hope

O merciful Lord,
bless with the first fruits of your mercy
the people who have waited long and remained faithful beyond hope.
Where pain has built a shield,
gently disarm the strength that has served its purpose,
and flood their lives with joy.
We pray for all people whose unmet yearning is known to you alone.
Give them the rich fruits of their steady, faithful love,
O Lord, we pray. Amen.

245. Unnoticed suffering

Lord God, you see the sparrow fall to the ground,
    unnoticed by people nearby.
We pray for all people who are falling through the cracks of life:
the vulnerable, the addicted, the sick and the confused,
    the lonely, the abused and the neglected.
Open our eyes to see the suffering and unmet needs on our doorsteps,
open our hearts to respond in appropriate ways,
and sustain the people and services that work
    to bind up the broken people of our world.
In the name of Jesus Christ we pray. Amen.

246. Lack of freedom

We pray, our Father, for people who, for whatever reason,
    do not know freedom:
for people, rightly or wrongly, behind bars,
for people who are locked inwardly by fears and obsessions,
for people who are a danger to themselves or to others,
for people who are controlled by others with malicious intent,
for people who are addicted to drugs, alcohol,
    gambling or any other dependency,
for people whose physical or mental needs limit their opportunities.
For these people, and for all others who lack
    the freedom you intend for your people, we pray,
asking that they may experience your liberating gospel in their lives.
We ask that such needs may be relieved through the actions of others.
In the name of Jesus Christ. Amen.

247. Families under pressure

We pray for families that are under pressure:
for people suffering the effects of broken relationships,
for people who are abused or ignored by those who should care for them,
for people torn from their families
    and those left behind who worry about them,
for families struggling with addiction, violence, crime or hatred,
for families shattered by bereavement.
Heavenly Father, bring hope and healing into shattered lives.
We pray this in the name of Jesus Christ, your Son, our Lord. Amen.

248. Children who are unsafe

We ask your protection, O loving Father,
    for all children who are unsafe in their homes or on their streets:
protect them from danger,
deliver them where they are already trapped or harmed,
provide them, we pray, with adults they can trust
to provide the support they need to develop
    into healthy and happy young people.
We pray in the name of Jesus Christ our Lord. Amen.

249. Young people at risk

Protect, O Lord, children and young people
whose wellbeing is at risk, for any reason,
from falling through the gaps in support
provided by families or public services.
We pray for young people whose homes are dangerous or inadequate,
and for those being sucked into gangs, addictions or crime.
As we pray for national and local government
    in setting and implementing policy,
we give thanks for the dedicated work of so many people
    who are committed to the welfare of young people
    and pray that their work will be increasingly effective.
We pray this in your name, Lord Jesus. Amen.

250. Parents whose dreams for their children are shattered

When our dreams for those we love lie shattered at our feet,
and we feel the piercing of a sword in our souls,
then, O Lord, give us the deep courage
to remain faithful through events that feel so unreal.
We pray particularly for parents facing the
    shreds and tatters of their dreams for their children,
the unanswered question whether they could have done more,
even the humiliation of being their parents.
Provide for them, O God our Father,
the wise counsel and practical support of people
who can stay with them amidst this horror and assure them
that, as you watched with Mary when your Son hung upon the cross,
    you know their names,
and you are alongside them in this hour of their distress.
We pray this in the name of Jesus Christ,
who bore such humiliation through his death. Amen.

251. Unmet needs

We pray for people with no one to care for them in their unmet needs.
Show us how we can respond,
with our time, our resources or our prayers,
and provoke us to active love and service of the people
    whom you put us in a position to serve.
We pray this in the name of Jesus Christ our Lord. Amen.

252. Needs we ignore

Attune our senses, Lord Jesus, to the difficult cry of the poor.
As you heard the cry of Bartimaeus, of the lepers,
and felt the touch of the woman who dared not stand in front of you,
so make us sensitive to the needs we can too easily brush past,
and dare us to stop and find out how we can help.
In your name we pray. Amen.

253. Neglected compassion

Forgive us, O Lord, when our compassion becomes absent-minded,
when we forget the concerns which once fired our action
and neglect the need for merciful attention.
Remind us today of situations that should continue
    to demand our attentive prayer and action
and lead us back into faithful response.
In the name of Jesus Christ. Amen.

254. Sensitivity to need

At times when tragedy fills the news and preoccupies us,
forgive us, O Lord,
for overlooking the lesser sorrows and sadnesses of people's lives.
Keep us attentive to the daily concerns of people around us,
give us the sensitivity to recognize when distress runs deep,
and fill us with the grace to respond with compassion and care.
We pray in the name of Jesus Christ our Lord. Amen.

255. Fragile lives

Show us, gentle God,
how to honour the fragility of so many people's lives.
Help us to tread softly with the vulnerable,
and to show kindness to the lonely or neglected.
Teach us to value their lives as precious and their needs
    as essential as those of the powerful and famous.
O tender Lord, use our hands and hearts as instruments of your peace.
We pray in your name, Lord Jesus. Amen.

256. Sources of hope and help

Gracious God, we pray for people who feel they
    have nowhere to turn in their distress.
Lead them to sources of hope and help.
Bless the ministry of cathedrals and churches
which remain open as beacons of hope and sanctuary,
and the work of agencies and charities that can provide
    a listening ear or resources of support and care.
Increase our sensitivity to people we encounter who bear
    unmet needs and make us messengers of grace.
For the sake of Jesus Christ our Lord. Amen.

257. Wilderness and storm

God of the wilderness,
sometimes it seems that you hide in the barren places,
and we feel we have lost our way.
God of the storm,
sometimes it is hard to hear your voice
above the chaos and the noise.
O holy, intimate God,
may all people know your presence
and the touch of your healing hands
amidst the turmoil and the desolation of our lives.
We pray in the name of Jesus Christ our Lord. Amen.

258. All kinds of need

Forgive us, Lord, when our prayers are like shopping lists
that put into inadequate words all the things we think the world needs.
Deliver us from the presumption that we know what is best
and instead lead us to trust in your great love for the world.
In peaceful faith help us to entrust our worries
    and concerns to your care.
We bring to you the people and needs we fret about
as well as those that are beyond our knowledge
and ask you to tend them all with your healing love.
In your name we pray, Lord Jesus. Amen.

259. Unspoken prayers

We pray, dear Lord, with and for people
who cannot put their prayers into words:
for needs spoken and unspoken,
for hearts that feel they are breaking with the weight of their burdens,
for howls of desolation that go unheard by others,
and for silenced lives that dare not voice their yearnings.
O Lord, who saw the sparrow fall,
    in the silence we hold before you all who fall unnoticed today.
[a few moments of silence]
Bless them and tend their wounds, we pray.
O Holy Spirit, intercede for them with sighs too deep for words. Amen.

People in poverty

260. Poverty

For people who cannot make ends meet, we pray, O God.
Where children suffer,
protect them from hindered development.
Where parents are depressed and feel they have failed their children,
enable them to find practical support and affirmation.
Where eviction looms,
guide people through the bureaucratic systems
    to adequate temporary accommodation;
and where they are forced to sleep rough,
protect them from dangers,
and help them access the services that are available.
In the face of increasing demands,
we pray for the work of foodbanks, Shelter,
    the Salvation Army and other charities,
and for the work of local authorities and statutory agencies.
In the name of Jesus Christ. Amen.

261. People with inadequate housing

God our Father, as we thank you for our own homes and families,
we pray for people who have no one or nowhere to call their own:
for those who sleep on our streets or in night shelters,
for prisoners who are released without a home to go to,
for people who live in condemned or inadequate housing,
for people who have been evicted and have not found alternative shelter,
and for all whose housing is unsuitable for a life of dignity and security.
We pray too for people who work to provide or manage good housing.
In the name of Jesus Christ. Amen.

262. Hunger

We bring before you, O Lord,
all people who have no one with whom to share a meal:
those who have no friends and those who have no food.
As we remember that you took bread and shared it with your friends,
enlarge our generosity,
so that no one we meet may hunger for food or fellowship.
Unlock our purses,
so that friends we do not know may break their bread together.
In the name of Jesus Christ we pray. Amen.

263. Foodbanks

Lord Jesus, you fed crowds who had no food.
When we consider the growing demand for foodbanks,
we are appalled that there can be food poverty in our country;
and we pray that your example will guide our response.
We pray for people whose normal pattern of life has been so disrupted
that they have had to ask for help;
may they find the food they need given to them
     with the respect that restores a sense of dignity.
We pray for people whose benefits are delayed
     or do not cover all their needs;
may they find compassion and support in their predicament.
Guide the staff and volunteers at foodbanks in their work,
and stir us all to be generous donors to our neighbours in their need.
In your name we pray, Lord Jesus. Amen.

264. Debt

O Lord God, who provided for the remission of debts
    in the year of Jubilee,
we pray for people and families who have become locked into debt
    and feel trapped in its clutches,
through lost or inadequate income, delayed benefits,
addictions or unwise spending.
Provide for them the support that they need
to resolve their current issues and avoid future debt.
We pray for debt counsellors, financial advisers,
and all who teach young people how to handle money wisely.
In the name of Jesus Christ our Lord. Amen.

People who are overwhelmed, in despair or grieving

265. Lost hope after disaster

Father, hear us as we pray for people whose hopes and dreams
    have been burned in fire and lie in ashes at their feet,
have been washed or blown away by natural disaster,
have been destroyed by malicious action;
or have vanished in economic disaster.
Come amidst their grief and crying,
and from the ruins restore new life and hope,
as we offer ourselves in your and their service. Amen.

266. Hope and healing

When anguished lives are at breaking point,
when violence stabs or loneliness becomes despair,
Lord Jesus, bring your healing balm.
When silence is a protective mask,
when lies unfold and substitute for the unspeakable truth,
Lord Jesus, bring your word of life.
When hearts are numbed with pain,
when fears overwhelm and comfort lies in oblivion,
Lord Jesus, bring your touch of grace.
Lord Jesus, make your Church a place
where hope, embodied, brings forth new hope,
so that lives that have been destroyed, abused and shamed
can be redeemed and healed.
In your name we pray. Amen.

267. Confusion and distress

When people's lives are turned upside down in a terrible instant,
come among them, O Lord, as rock and salvation.
When they are stunned, numb or uncomprehending,
breathe gently on their sorrow with your breath of life.
As they seek other people for help and support,
hold them all safe in the midst of the fire and tempest of their turmoil.
We pray this in the name of Jesus Christ our Lord. Amen.

268. Grief

O Lord, our Shepherd,
you walk with us through the valley of the shadow of death.
We pray for people for whom to live is to grieve
   and to endure unbearable sorrow.
Wipe the tears from streaming eyes,
calm the terror of loss and suffering,
and speak peace deep in hearts that are breaking.
Where the causes of suffering can be curbed,
empower those who work to do so;
and where the suffering must be borne,
grant resilience and the comfort
that you walk with your people amidst their grief.
Lead us all, we pray, to the still waters of refreshment.
In the name of Jesus Christ, our Good Shepherd. Amen.

269. People who grieve

O tender Lord, we turn to you when we are weighed down by grief.
You wept at the tomb of your friend Lazarus.
Come alongside all who grieve, *especially* . . .
Comfort them with your gentle presence,
and give them peace amidst their confusion and sorrow.
In your name we pray. Amen.

270. People needing solace

Comfort, O loving God, all people who need solace and consolation
if they are to face the demands of their life,
especially those we now name before you in the silence of our hearts;
help them to access the support they need,
and make us willing to be an answer to our prayer.
In the name of Jesus Christ our Lord. Amen.

271. People who yearn for hope

When yearning for wellbeing aches unremittingly,
and longing for wholeness seeps into the crevices
    of lives deadened by the pain of reality,
may seeds of hope be sown to sustain the weary and the grieving,
and may consciences be pricked into action in the places of prosperity.
We pray this, O holy God,
whose kingdom will come on earth as it is in heaven,
in the name of Jesus Christ our Lord. Amen.

272. Despair

We pray, O compassionate God,
for people who live with an ambient sense of despair:
for those whose circumstances give them good reason to despair,
we pray for the support and help they need,
for those who live with unspecific fear or anxiety,
we pray for a lifting of their spirits and light in their shadowed places,
for all people whose minds and spirits are weighed down or troubled,
we pray for your pervasive grace to penetrate the
    deep isolation that despair can bring.
Inspire them with your gentle yet strong hope and assurance
    of your presence walking alongside them day by day.
We pray this in the name of Jesus Christ our Lord. Amen.

273. Tears

Lord Jesus, you wept at Lazarus's grave, in Gethsemane,
    and when you looked over Jerusalem.
We bring to you the tears that have been wept in your world
    (*in this cathedral / church / hospital / prison / . . .*) today,
the tears wept in pain, in anger, in frustration,
the tears wept in sorrow, in grief, in despair,
and the tears of joy, amazement and exhilaration.
Lord Jesus, bless kindly all who have wept today. Amen.

274. Grief and confusion

Lord Jesus, unseen companion on the Emmaus Road,
walk beside us in our grief and pain,
our confusion and broken hearts.
Stay with us as we voice our deepest fears and disappointed dreams.
Still the doubts that rise and speak the peace we long to hear.
In your name we pray. Amen.

275. People who grieve without hope

When death has ripped lives apart,
or grief is interrupted and cannot run its course,
then, O risen Lord, amidst the confusion
speak words of comfort and of peace.
Bring the reassurance of your risen presence
and your continuing assurance that broken lives
can be given new hope and purpose.
We pray for people who grieve without hope;
breathe into their sorrow the fresh air of your life.
We pray in your name, O Lord. Amen.

276. The loneliness and disorientation of grief

As you met with Mary, weeping in the garden,
Lord Jesus, come alongside bereft people who, in their disorientation,
do not expect to find you alongside them.
Surprise them gently as you absorb their angry questions,
invade their death with life,
call them by their name,
and send them out with joy and good news to proclaim.
We pray this in your name. Amen.

277. The death of a baby

We pray, dear Father, for all families who grieve the death of a baby.
Be present to them in their sorrow.
Give them peace in their distress
and the assurance that their loved child is safe in your loving care.
We pray in the name of Jesus Christ our Lord,
who called the children to him and blessed them. Amen.

278. People who grieve

We pray for people whose grief and loss
   make them feel that they are limping through life
or engaging with the world from behind an opaque window.
Lord Jesus, as you brought freedom to people who turned to you,
so now, we pray that your Holy Spirit will bring liberation
   to people who feel in any way bound by grief today.
We pray this in your name. Amen.

279. Living with the fear of death

O risen Lord, we worship you:
through your death the power of death is destroyed
and by your glorious resurrection life and immortality are brought to light.
We pray for people everywhere who live in fear of death,
from war, violence, substance abuse, famine,
or from lack of hope in your resurrection.
We pray for all who work to bring freedom from fear in any of its guises,
and we pray that, through their labours,
your salvation may be known throughout the world.
Lord, make us instruments of your peace, we pray. Amen.

280. Regret

O heavenly Father,
we pray for people who live with the terrible consequences
of a decision or action years ago which they now deeply regret
and which has blighted their lives ever since.
As they look back with self-reproach or anger at what they have lost,
desperation at their current circumstances and despair for the future,
we pray that you will break into their lives
with the assurance of your transforming presence
in the midst of the hopelessness.
We pray, too, for the work of all agencies that can help people
    whose past has such a cruel grip on their future.
We pray this in the name of Jesus Christ,
who brought freedom to all who turned to him. Amen.

281. Destroyed dreams

When it feels as though a stone has been rolled
    across the tomb of our hopes,
        leaving us alone to dash our dreams against it,
then, O Lord, give us the courage to step out
    and find that we can walk with you
        through this new territory of disappointment
        into the light of a new and unimagined dawn.
In the name of Jesus Christ our Lord. Amen.

282. Facing emergencies and life's nightmares

O Lord, when life spins out of control
and suddenly what seemed predictable becomes unpredictable,
grant your peace and serenity to all who are affected.
We pray for people facing emergencies or situations
    that are their worst nightmare,
yet now have become relentless reality.
Especially today we pray for people caught up in . . .
Draw them into the vastness of your love and care for them,
and, in the midst of whirling emotions,
make your presence known with tenderness and strength.
We pray that they will be reached with sources of help and support,
and that they will know your peace that passes all understanding.
In the name of Jesus Christ our Lord. Amen.

283. Earthquakes in life

We pray, Lord God, for people who feel that they
    are living through an earthquake of life
and that the ground that was once secure is
    now slipping from under them.
When they are trapped in the tangle of a world
    they once moved through with ease,
then, O God, break through the impenetrable walls
    of shattered expectations and ruined dreams,
moving freely and bringing life,
as once you did when you spoke the simple and
    creative words, "Let there be light." Amen.

284. The storms of life

When it feels as though our lives are being torn apart,
when there is no consolation and all seems darkness and confusion,
then, dear Lord, attune our ears to hear your voice
calling to us by name over the sound of the storm and tempest.
Reach out to us with your welcoming arms, O Lord,
and grant us your peace.
We pray this not only for ourselves,
but for all people who are overwhelmed
   by the storms and whirlwinds of life.
We pray in the name of our Lord Jesus Christ,
who walked over the stormy waters to reach his fearful friends. Amen.

285. The storms of life*

To you, O Lord, we turn, in the midst of the storms of life.
In our weakness, please uphold us and lead us to new strength
through trusting, peaceful quietness.
Reveal to us again love's meaning
and teach us afresh that all shall be well, ah, yes, all shall be well.
We pray this in the name of Jesus Christ our courteous Lord. Amen.

286. Tragedy

When tragedy strikes and a howl of anguish is heard
in the face of appalled, unbounded despair,
when family and friends are left with nothing
but the broken bodies of those they have loved,
when trust in your love is undermined
and there is no way to make any sense of what has happened,
then, O God, give us the courage to stay alongside the grieving.
Help us not to offer pat answers but to be witnesses, like Mary,
   of your power to bring new life and hope when all we can see is death.
We pray this in the name of Jesus Christ,
whose broken body was held by anguished women. Amen.

---

*   Based on words of Julian of Norwich

Sickness and suffering

287. Healing

God of hope and healing,
you are always turning lives around,
rewriting stories and turning life's losses into gains:
we bring ourselves and our loved ones
and ask you to heal, make whole, and breathe new life.
Then inspire us to be your agents of healing in the world,
we pray this in the name of Jesus Christ,
who healed the sick and restored hope. Amen.

288. Healing

Lord Jesus, many who were sick and dying
    owed their healing to your care.
As once you healed those who were broken,
forgave those who had sinned, and mended tormented lives,
we pray for all who follow in your healing footsteps:
for the healing ministry of the Church,
for doctors, nurses, therapists and care workers,
for hospital administrators and support staff,
for the emergency services and social services,
and for all who care for relatives and friends in their homes.
May each one be an instrument of your healing
and a means of blessing to the sick and needy.
In your name we pray, Amen.

289. Pain

Risen Lord Jesus, you endured the pain of human suffering.
Be present with all people who today struggle with relentless pain,
and through the kindness of others
grant to them a glimpse of hope and joy.
Bless and strengthen those who, in this *city / town / hospital / hospice. . .*
work to bring relief to others.
Grant skill to doctors and nurses,
and compassion to all who offer care.
We ask this in your name. Amen.

290. Women in labour

Lord Jesus, you were born of a woman who knew the pain of labour.
We pray for women today who are waiting to give birth
   and are crying their child into the world:
for all who are fearful or apprehensive
and those whose pain seems unbearable,
for those with inadequate medical support in places of danger,
or who are entirely on their own.
Lord Jesus, as your mother once gazed into your newborn eyes with love,
so protect mothers and babies today
as they anticipate the joy of seeing each other face to face for the first time.
We pray this in your name. Amen.

291. Children who are sick

Lord Jesus, you went readily to the bedside of a dying little girl
   and restored her life.
We pray for babies and children who are seriously ill or dying,
and who suffer pain or distress
because of what is happening to them;
for their parents who, like Jairus in your day,
   have run out of ways to help
and need to rely on the care of medical services;
for families as they cope with the disruption to routines
   and the impact on young siblings;
and for the medical staff providing the treatment and care.
In such tragic and demanding contexts we pray, O Lord,
that your love will be tangible, and that your healing presence
   will bring calm to ease fear and hope and to relieve distress.
We pray in your name, O loving Lord. Amen.

292. Mental health concerns

We pray, O compassionate Lord,
   for people who struggle with mental health issues,
   their own or those of people they love.
As we pray for their wellbeing and peace,
   we ask that you help us to strengthen our commitment as a society
   to secure adequate resources for mental health services.
Increase our understanding of the miraculous complexity
   of our bodies, minds and spirits,
and guide all who are developing or delivering resources
   that bring help and healing.
We pray this in your name, Lord Jesus. Amen.

293. Mental health concerns

We pray, O Lord, for people who live with poor mental health:
for those whose stories are splashed across the headlines,
giving them publicity that they desire or dread,
and for the much greater number of unknown people
    who struggle on their own or within their families,
particularly for those who do not have the support that they need
for themselves or for those they love who suffer.
When people are lonely, despairing or suicidal,
we pray that you will provide people and places of comfort and safety.
Inspire and strengthen all who work to support and improve
    the mental wellbeing of others.
We ask this in the name of Jesus Christ our Lord. Amen.

294. People who are confused

We pray for people in care homes and nursing homes
who are confused by their surroundings,
and fear they have been forgotten.
Speak through their distress your healing words of calm,
and where their memory is confused, shed rays of light and clarity.
Comfort their families, who grieve their confusion,
and give wisdom and patience to their carers.
We ask this in the name of Jesus Christ our Lord. Amen.

295. Dementia

We pray for all people affected by dementia in any of its forms:
for people who are aware of reductions in their memories,
language or problem-solving skills,
and fear where this is leading,
for people whose needs go unnoticed by themselves or others
and are unmet until there is a crisis,
for their families as they adjust to unwelcome changes to the personality
    of a loved one and their new needs for care and support,
and for carers, at home or in care homes,
particularly when the demands on them exceed their inner resources.
We thank you, Lord, for the research and support that is available,
and we pray that people who do not have access to resources
    for a happy and dignified way of life
may find the care and assistance they need.
We pray in the name of Jesus Christ our Lord. Amen.

296. Memories

We pray, O God, for people who look back with regret:
for old people with long and sometimes lonely memories,
for the confused with difficult and sometimes unreliable memories,
for families with difficult and sometimes painful memories,
for unloved people with sad and sometimes aching memories,
for the abused with traumatic and sometimes unendurable memories.
For all people whose regrets for the past silence their hopes for the future,
grant your healing and your peace, O loving God. Amen.

297. Long illness

Lord Jesus, bless with your healing presence all people
   who are affected by interminable illness,
those who suffer from it and those who care for them.
We pray for people who know that their illness is incurable,
help them to find their peace with you
   in the midst of the increasing restrictions of their lives.
We pray too for people whose diagnosis is uncertain
   and who do not know how long their illness will last,
or whether any treatment is possible.
Give skill to doctors in diagnosing and treating long-term illness,
relief from painful symptoms for those who suffer from it,
and patience and comfort to everyone whose lives are affected by it.
We ask this in your name, O Lord. Amen.

298. Incurable disease

Bless, O Lord, all people who live with incurable degenerative disease
which gradually eats away at their independence
   and reduces their quality of life.
We pray for their families, who watch them lose control of their bodies
and have to provide increasing levels of personal care
or accept that expectations of family life must yield to care-home life;
for medical researchers who seek to reduce the impact of such diseases,
and for friends and colleagues who feel powerless to help.
In the midst of life-changing illness, O God,
shed your light and peace,
   and enable people to bring joy out of sorrow and difficulty.
In the name of Jesus Christ. Amen.

299. Terminal illness or living with unmeetable needs*

Be present, O gracious God, with people whose needs cannot be met
    and who cry in vain for their thirst to be quenched.
As the people they love pour out their souls on their behalf,
bear aching memories of former times of joy,
or cry to you in their confusion,
renew for all of them the awareness of your steadfast love,
and sing your songs of faithfulness to them.
O Lord, refresh them with your living water. Amen.

300. Long-term illness

In the face of long-term, unrelenting illness that simply persists,
    sapping the endurance of patients, families and carers,
we pray for strength to carry on,
not only for the sick but for all who tend them.
Give them the patience to continue caring and being cared for,
the stamina to face the endless routine,
the gentleness to nurse well,
and the words to encourage each other day by day.
Be present at such bedsides with your gracious touch,
Lord Jesus Christ, we pray. Amen.

301. Long-term treatment

Lord God, our healer, we pray for all people who face an ongoing
    regimen of treatment as an inpatient or an outpatient:
give them stamina to cope with the treatment and its side effects,
support as they make adjustments to their lifestyles,
protection from germs and viruses,
patience for the long haul
and a successful outcome to their treatment.
We ask this in the name of Jesus Christ. Amen.

---

*   Based on Psalm 42

302. The impact of sickness

Lord Jesus, healer of the sick,
who also endured the long and searing pain of the cross,
we pray for people whose illness seems interminable
or whose pain is unrelenting,
making it easy to become crotchety.
We pray too for the people who care for the sick at home,
especially where family life is disrupted
and the tediousness of it all seems overwhelming.
Bring your healing peace into their midst we pray. Amen.

People who respond to need

303. Compassionate people

For people who have not run out of kindness
or despaired of their limited influence
but carry on in their service of others,
we give you thanks, O God.
May they be our example in the service of your people
and, in turn, make us into examples of the goodness
that is not daunted by the seeming smallness of what we can do.
We pray in the name of Jesus Christ,
who sent such unlikely people to turn the world upside down. Amen.

304. Nurses

Lord Jesus, who healed the sick,

(on this International Nurses Day*)

we give you thanks and pray for nurses around the world
who continue your work of healing and care.
In this country, we give you thanks for the work of the NHS
    and its staff and volunteers,
and we pray for its wise resourcing and management.
We pray for nurses who put themselves at risk for the sake of the sick,
especially those who work under the threat of war or terrorism,
or are doing their best with inadequate facilities.
Give to all nurses the skill, the patience and the compassion
    they need to serve your people,
and grant them great joy in their healing work.
In your name we pray. Amen.

305. Medical research

We give you thanks, O God,
for the skills and patience of those who work in medical research.
Prosper their work for the good of all people,
and lead them to new resources for the relief of pain,
control of viruses and disease,
and the healing of sickness.
We pray this, O Lord, in the name of Jesus Christ our Lord. Amen.

---

*   12 May

306. Hospices

Bless, O Lord, the work of hospices.
We give thanks for the care they offer to the terminally ill and dying.
We pray for their residents, day patients
and all the families who look to the hospice for care and support.
We pray for the staff and volunteers,
who work to make them places of safety and peace in troubling times.
We ask that your grace and joy will prevail,
and that all who enter their doors will find
    unexpected and lasting blessing.
In the name of Jesus Christ our Lord. Amen.

307. Watching with those who are dying

Be present, O gracious God, with people who watch, wait and care
while their partner, parent, child or friend is suffering and dying.
We pray for people whose memories of years of love bubble up
both to bless and sear their hearts,
for people whose feelings are confused or guilty
as pent-up frustration or dislike meet the anticipation of an ending,
for people who are simply exhausted,
who find it hard to let go or long for release,
or who fear the future on their own.
Amidst these complex and interwoven emotions
bring your peace and hope, we pray, O God. Amen.

308. The caring professions

Strengthen and equip all people, we pray,
who see misery and despair at close quarters
    and work to ameliorate their impact.
We pray for social workers, health workers, carers and counsellors,
    for the police and emergency services,
local government staff and members, for foodbank workers,
    the prison and probation services,
the NSPCC, Age Concern, the Salvation Army,
    the RSPCA and similar organizations,
for . . . and for all good neighbours.
Prosper their commitment and work for the good of people
    who cannot help themselves.
In the name of Jesus Christ our Lord. Amen.

309. Carers

We thank you, gracious God,
for the example of kindness and compassion
shown by care workers in families, homes and in care homes.
Bless them in their daily care of people who depend on them.
Give them patience and humour, skill and gentleness,
safety in their travel between people's homes
    and fulfilment in their service of others.
We pray in the name of Jesus Christ our Lord. Amen.

310. Carers and medical staff

We pray, O Lord, for people who care for others
and must juggle anti-social working hours
   with their own and their families' needs.
Grant them times of refreshment and renewal together.
We pray for people who put their own lives at risk
in order to provide care in times of stress or high demand.
Keep them safe from infection or other harm.
Renew the energy and focus of medical staff
who work long hours on complex operations.
We pray for care workers and nurses
who wash patients, clean up messes,
   and provide essential human contact.
Give them compassion, a sense of humour and fulfilment in their work.
All this we pray in the name of Jesus Christ our Lord. Amen.

311. People who care

Good Shepherd of your people,
we give you thanks for gentle hands and caring hearts
which embody your care today in places of sorrow and distress.
Bless all people who are in a place to give human expression to divine love.
In your name we pray. Amen.

312. Caring for others

Teach us, dear Lord, how to be caring in our care for others,
attentive to their wishes,
patient with their demands,
quick to respond to their lead,
and slow to impose our own solutions on them.
We pray that our relationships and communities
will be marked by gladness in responding to each other's needs.
In the name of Jesus Christ our Lord. Amen.

313. Respect for others

As we live together in your world, O Lord,
stiffen our respect for others,
especially those whose dignity has been demeaned,
make us supple in our response to their needs,
that they may find us ready to help
and to nudge them into new hope and trust in your goodness.
We pray this for the sake of Jesus Christ our Lord. Amen.

314. Action for those who suffer

O Lord our God, make us into people of stubborn action
on behalf of the poor, the forgotten and the outcast.
Prosper the work of charities and aid agencies
that go into places others dare not visit or prefer to forget;
keep their workers safe from harm
and make them beacons of hope to the people they serve.
Challenge us regularly about our financial support
for people for whom life is untenable in its present form,
and make us intractable in our advocacy
for seeing beyond our own wants and needs in life.
We pray in the name of Jesus Christ our Lord,
who never turned from the love and service of people in need. Amen.

315. Commitment to people in need

Draw out of us, O Lord, new depths of commitment,
more attentive and generous responses to the needs of others,
and new willingness to go beyond the realms
    of the familiar and the secure.
Make us thoughtful and daring in our discipleship,
and help us to bring your good news to a world that is hurting.
In your name, we pray, Lord Jesus. Amen.

316. Volunteers who make a difference

Thank you, O God our Father, for all people
who make a difference for good in our local communities.
We pray for older people who volunteer their time and skills,
for children whose enthusiasm for environmental issues inspires us all,
for families who include other people's children in their activities,
for good neighbours and attentive neighbourhood workers
    who notice and respond to people in need.
We pray, too, for isolated people
and those whose needs appear to go unnoticed and unmet.
Build us, together, into neighbourhood communities
of care and compassion,
hope and inspiration.
We pray in the name of Jesus Christ. Amen.

317. People who make a difference

We praise and thank you, Lord God,
for the people who make a difference for good in the lives of others:
for those who care for people who very elderly and disabled,
for people who teach new skills to young people,
for teachers who light fires of wonder and inquisitiveness
    in the minds of their pupils,
for people whose contribution is never acknowledged
but lives in the memory of the people they inspired,
for the people who have made a difference in our lives.
May they be our inspiration and example
as we offer ourselves to make a difference in your world today.
We pray in the name of Jesus Christ. Amen.

CREATION

The wonder of creation

318. The wonder of creation
For the wonders of creation,
the earth and sky,
the stars and seas,
the worlds beyond our sight of outer space and subatomic particle,
and the ever-changing newness that you bring,
we give you thanks, O Lord.
Holy Spirit, breathe your life into our hearts
and make us wise and responsible in our wonder at this world. Amen.

319. Creation's praise
We rejoice, O God, in the symphony that nature
plays to you, its creator and sustainer.
Tune our hearts to its melodies and harmonies,
and teach us to join in the songs of praise that echo
    from sky and sea, mountain and pasture,
so that we may be responsible and joyful stewards of your world. Amen.

320. The wonder of the world
For the beauty of the earth, the skies
and the oceans in all their lavish richness,
for the vivacity of movement and the silence of stillness,
for the palette of colours and the ever-changing sparkle of light,
for the sounds and echoes of space and the whisper of ruffled leaves,
for all the wonders of your world,
accept our thanks and praise, O glorious God. Amen.

321. The world's unexpected delights

Keep surprising us, O joyful God,
with the unexpected and spontaneous signs
of your delight in your world
in all its wonder and its awesome mystery.
Stretch our minds and hearts
with the unveiling of your glory in creation.
We pray in the name of Jesus Christ. Amen.

322. The wonder of the world

For the rush of glory that cascades down hillsides of bluebells,
that arcs above us in rainbows,
that fills the air with the fragrance of sweet peas,
that echoes from tree to tree with birdsong,
that crunches beneath our feet as we scuff through autumn leaves,
that silences and beautifies cities in a wrap of snowfall,
for glory that glows from season to season,
we bring you our awed gratitude, O holy God. Amen.

323. The beauty of the seasons

For the sheer beauty of creation on a *spring / summer / autumn / winter* day
    and the privilege of experiencing it,
we give you our thanks and praise, O God.
Teach us to notice the passing of the seasons
and to wonder at the magnificence of the glory you lay before us
in the daily changes of nature.
In our enjoyment, show us how we can be wise stewards
    of your wonderful world. Amen.

324. Beauty and creativity

Inspire us, O artist God,

when we wonder at the beauty of the universe you have made,

to create beauty wherever we can,

and to appreciate beauty when we encounter it in unexpected places.

Excite us with the possibilities and potentiality

    of the creativity you have given us.

We pray in the name of Jesus Christ. Amen.

325. The changing seasons

For the particular glories of each season

and the paced transience of each daily unfolding

we offer our thanks and praise, O creative God.

Warm our hearts with wonder and expand our gratitude

    for the beauty of the familiar newness. Amen.

326. Weather

Thank you, Lord, for the variety of weather we experience

    and the resulting glory of creation which provides

our food, water, wind power, gardens and countryside.

We pray for people for whom the *(current)* weather makes life difficult

and who have inadequate resources to deal with it,

for people whose homes and livelihoods are threatened

by storms, drought, floods, extreme cold or extreme heat,

and for people who can only see the changing weather from indoors.

Lord, open our ears, eyes, noses and fingers

to experience the wonder of the weather

and teach us to be grateful even when it rains on our picnic. Amen.

327. Gardens

Creator God, who first gardened the world for Adam to tend,
we praise you for the beauty of gardens,
the pollen that nurtures bees and butterflies,
the fragrance of flowers that delights our senses,
and the fruit and vegetables that feed and sustain us.
We pray for people who can never enjoy a garden,
especially for the millions who live in squalor
and whose only outlook each day
is bleak, desolate, dangerous, or demeaning of the human spirit.
Make us kind gardeners of your natural creation
and generous in our sharing of its benefits.
We pray in the name of Jesus Christ. Amen.

328. Sunsets

You stun us, O artistic God,
with the beauty of sunsets:
those evening blessings when pastel hazes erupt into life,
fuchsia and lemon dare to touch without clashing,
and the heavens declare the glory of God in ever-changing wonder
as your creativity is let loose on another canvas.
Lead us, O God, into deeper wonder
at the delights of these signs of your presence in our world,
and when darkness falls,
teach us to wait with eager expectation
that you will do it all over again tomorrow. Amen.

329. The night sky and space research

On those nights when the sky simply gorgeous,
is sparkling with stars, graced by a rich, full moon
or the slender delicacy of a new moon's curve,
then, O God our creator, lift our hearts in wonder and praise
for the mystery of time and space revealed above our heads.
Guide all who explore the unknown worlds beyond our sight,
and, in our probing of its wonders,
make all nations good stewards rather than litter-leavers.
Astonish and awe us into a right humility
    at the vastness of your creation.
In the name of Jesus Christ our Lord, we pray. Amen.

330. The Book of Nature

Lord Jesus, you knew that the heavens declare the glory of God,
and that the lilies of the field reveal your Father's loving care.
Teach us, as you taught your disciples,
to consider the small things of creation.
Slow us down and meet us in our attention to
    something as familiar as a flower or stone.
Open our ears, eyes and hearts, O Lord, we pray,
to learn from you in the Book of Nature. Amen.

331. Spring

"Nothing is so beautiful as spring":*
Seeing the early blackthorn balanced like snowflakes on hedgerows,
and the perfect clash of colours as flowers open;
we rejoice in your goodness, O Lord.
Hearing the exotic harmonies of the songs of birds,
the bandy-legged cavorting of lambs
and the dissonance of their conversation with their mothers,
all speaking of love in a language we cannot understand;
we rejoice in your goodness, O Lord.
Please open our eyes and ears to your glory revealed in creation,
and give us the exuberance of spring as we rejoice. Amen.

332. Autumn

When we scuff our feet
through heaps of leaves from left-over summer;
when we watch with pangs of admiration
the birds begin their long migration flights;
when dew falls overnight and we wake to the intricate
    beauty of glittering spiders' webs;
when days shorten, temperatures drop and harvests are over,
awe us with the beauty of endings
and prepare our hearts, Lord God,
for the sparser, more hard-won gifts of winter.
We pray this with thanksgiving
for the ripened gifts and blessings of autumn. Amen.

---

*   From "Spring" by Gerard Manley Hopkins

333. Animals

We bring great thanks, O Lord,

for the pets we love and cherish as companions in our lives.

Thank you for their trusting love, vivacious playfulness,

faithful friendship and companionable presence.

We pray for the work of vets,

of the RSPCA and similar organizations

which protect suffering or abandoned animals,

for organizations which train assistance or detection animals,

and for all working animals.

We pray this in the name of Jesus,

who rode on a donkey. Amen.

334. Walking in the countryside

Thank you, O God,

for all the public footpaths in the countryside

that open its delights to us when we ramble and explore.

We praise you for the sights, sounds and smells we pass;

both the vast views and vistas,

and the tiny insects, flora and fauna that could escape our attention.

Help us to walk with open ears and eyes

and to let creation lead us in a song of joy.

We pray this in the name of Jesus Christ our Lord,

who walked so many country paths. Amen.

STEWARDSHIP OF THE WORLD

Stewardship of the world

335. The world as gift

Open our hearts, O Lord,

to experience the world as gift.

Stir our wills to care for it well,

so that we can pass on the gift to future generations.

In the name of Jesus Christ our Lord. Amen.

336. Wise stewardship

O Lord, when we gasp in awe and wonder

   at the beauty of the world that you have made,

we lack the words for a fitting phrase to thank you,

so we pray that our enjoyment of it may be our praise.

When we ache as birdsong ceases, cattle die,

and drought, flood and forest-stripping cause suffering,

we lack the words to offer repentance

   for our greed and thoughtless actions.

so we pray that you will help us, O Lord,

in our resolve that our future living will be more loving,

expressed in wise stewardship of the world

   you have entrusted to our care.

We offer this prayer in the name of Jesus Christ our Lord. Amen.

337. Protecting creation

Amidst the beauty of creation with its exquisite and extravagant wonders,

may we know your beauty and presence, O Lord.

Amidst the ravages of creation,

forgive us our complacency and stir us into action

to restore that which is despoiled,

and safeguard that which is endangered.

We pray this, O God our Creator, in the name of Jesus Christ our Lord,

who knew your presence and care

when he considered the lilies of the field. Amen.

338. Stewardship of God's world

O God, our creator, we praise you for the glories of your creation,
for its smells and textures,
for its sights and sounds; for its diversity and its wonders.
In our grateful enjoyment of your good gifts
    make us wise stewards of your world,
and tenacious in helping those for whom the world
    is a harsh and unforgiving place,
be it through war, famine, natural disaster or exploitation.
We ask this in the name of Jesus Christ our Lord. Amen.

339. Exploring and caring for creation

God of creation, glorious in its scope and wondrous in its detail,
we give thanks for the skill of scientists,
    whose exploration of your world
    adds to our understanding and wonder.
Guide and inspire them in their work.
We also see your world torn and broken,
laid waste and abused by natural disaster, war and exploitation,
and so we pray for all who work for the wellbeing of the natural world,
and for wisdom in our stewardship and our use of its resources.
In the name of Jesus Christ our Lord. Amen.

340. The joy and despoliation of nature

Open our ears, O Lord, to the polyphony of joy and exultation
sung by creation in its beauty and life,
but do not dull our hearing to the discordant sounds
of spoiled lives and despoiled creation.
Teach us new descants and harmonies in our living
that celebrate all that is good
and work to resolve all that is out of joint
in our living in your world.
In the name of Jesus Christ. Amen.

LITANIES

341. Litany for daily life

O Lord God, hear us as we pray:
for your Church across the world;
for those you have called to Christian leadership;
and for all baptized people in their life and ministry.
Lord, in your mercy, hear our prayer.

For your world in its beauty and its shame;
for the leaders of the nations and all who serve
    in local and national government;
for the leaders of industry and commerce;
for all who work in health, emergency and social services;
and for all who suffer under usurped or corrupted power.
Lord, in your mercy, hear our prayer.

For our schools, colleges and universities;
for libraries, museums and cultural centres;
for people who work in sport, recreation and leisure industries;
for our local shops and businesses;
and those who keep our streets clean and our traffic moving.
Lord, in your mercy, hear our prayer.

For the sick and suffering;
for doctors, nurses, therapists and all who provide care for others;
for all who are homeless or inadequately housed;
for refugees, and all who feel out of place in their surroundings;
for those who are alone and whose needs are unmet.
Lord, in your mercy, hear our prayer.

For ourselves, our families and friends,
that we may live this day with joy and hope,
determination in the face of difficulty
and compassion in the face of need.
Lord, in your mercy, hear our prayer.

342. Long litany

O holy, blessed and glorious Trinity, one God:
Gracious God, hear our prayer.

We pray to you, O Holy God,
whom we desire and yet we fear,
whom we adore and yet we shun,
in our times of human need and agony,
of boundless joy and glorious hope,
of unsteady pilgrimage and uncertain trust:
Gracious God, hear our prayer.

In our times of want and times of wealth,
in our times of confusions and of confidence,
in our times of birth and death,
and in the day of judgement:
Gracious God, hear our prayer.

That you will build and guide your Church,
leading us in the ways of justice and of peace:
Gracious God, hear our prayer.

That this *cathedral / church* will be a holy place for all who come here;
that all who work or visit here
will be given inquiring minds and holy curiosity to pursue and love you:
Gracious God, hear our prayer.

That these buildings will echo with your presence,
shelter with your peace
and speak of your tender care:
Gracious God, hear our prayer.

That you will rule the hearts of world leaders
and all in authority in this and other lands,
that they may do justice, love mercy
and walk in the ways of truth:
Gracious God, hear our prayer.

That you will bring all wars to just and lasting peace,
restrain terrorists and protect the innocent,
bring all refugees to safety in their homelands,
and lead all nations in the pursuit of unity and peace:
Gracious God, hear our prayer.

That you will protect this nation and this city
from violence and crime on our streets,
from child abuse and domestic violence in our homes,
and from greed and corruption in our institutions:
Gracious God, hear our prayer.

That you will show pity on all prisoners, hostages and captives,
all who are homeless or hungry,
and all who are desolate or oppressed:
Gracious God, hear our prayer.

That you will watch over all who travel,
all whose work is dangerous or demeaning,
and all whose environment is unhealthy:
Gracious God, hear our prayer.

That you will bless and protect your people,
tending the sick, solacing the suffering,
showing mercy to the afflicted, giving rest to the exhausted,
blessing the dying and protecting the joyful:
Gracious God, hear our prayer.

That you will bind up the brokenhearted
and those whose spirits are crushed,
those who howl in pain
and those silenced by despair:
Gracious God, hear our prayer.

That you will bring to safety those who stray
and guide our feet into the way of truth:
Gracious God, hear our prayer.

That we will be faithful to do the work you have given us to do:
We pray you, hear us, Lord of love.

That you will give us hearts to love and fear you
with passion and reverence, tenderness and trust:
We pray you, hear us, Lord of love.

That you will keep us from contentment
with anything less than your life-giving gifts
and graces let loose in the world:
We pray you, hear us, Lord of love.

That you will comfort all who mourn:
We pray you, hear us, Lord of love.

That you will grant to all the faithful departed eternal life and peace:
We pray you, hear us, Lord of love.

That you will grant us, in the fellowship of (. . .) *and* all the saints,
to attain to your heavenly kingdom:
We pray you, hear us, Lord of love.

O Lamb of God, you take away the sins of the world,
Have mercy upon us.
O Lamb of God, you take away the sins of the world,
Have mercy upon us.
O Lamb of God, you take away the sins of the world,
Grant us your peace.

Lord, have mercy upon us,
Christ, have mercy upon us,
Lord, have mercy upon us.

343. Litany for the world
O holy God, you search us out and know us:
in your compassion forgive our offences
and do not reward us according to our sins;
in your redeeming power create and make in us new and contrite hearts.
Have mercy upon us.

O holy God, Creator of heaven and earth,
you spoke and worlds came to be,
you blessed your creation and called it good:
astound us afresh with your life and goodness.
Creator God, hear our prayer.

You formed us in your image,
and called us to care for your creation:
help us in our stewardship to be creative and compassionate,
fruitful and faithful,
that your earth may break forth into song.
Creator God, hear our prayer.

You led your people out of bondage,
forming a people for yourself to love and serve you:
heal us from hardness of heart and refusal to love,
and from contempt of your Word spoken among us.
Creator God, hear our prayer.

You sent your prophets to recall your people to your paths:
keep us from compromise or complacency in the face of evil,
and kindle in us your passion for justice and truth.
Creator God, hear our prayer.

O holy God, Redeemer of the world,
you took fragile human flesh,
born as one of us:
by your obedience to God's word,
by your baptism, fasting and temptation:
Incarnate God, deliver us.

You healed the sick, fed the hungry and reached out to those in need:
from the callousness that closes our hearts in the face of suffering,
and from the terror of another person's need that tempts us to withdraw:
Incarnate God, deliver us.

You called Zacchaeus to be your friend
and saw the widow's costly gift:
from meanness of spirit and lack of generosity,
from the fear that in giving we will go in need,
and from possessiveness of this world's goods:
Incarnate God, deliver us.

By your agony and delight in choosing to do the will of God,
by your cross and passion,
by your brutal death,
by your world-shattering resurrection and ascension:
Incarnate God, deliver us.

O Holy Spirit, Sanctifier of the faithful,
you swept over the face of deep waters,
God's presence in the formless void:
O breath of God, pierce our chaos and breathe life.
Come among us, bearing life.

You came in burning bush, in still small voice,
as dove, as tongues of fire:
surprising God, ever unpredictable and uncontained,
come, startle and sustain us.
Come among us, bearing life.

You drove Jesus into the wilderness,
filled him with power to bring good news:
lead us where we would not go,
disturb us with unsettling life,
and rest upon us with your peace.
Come among us, bearing life.

344. Litany for creation

Creator God,
you have formed a world of beauty and delight,
of immense wonder and microscopic detail.
Creator God, we bring our praise.

Creator God,
you have formed a world of mountains and lakes,
of skies and oceans, rivers and deserts,
forests and gardens.
Creator God, we bring our praise.

Creator God,
you formed a world beyond our sight,
of space beyond our comprehension
and galaxies beyond our dreaming.
Creator God, we bring our praise.

Creator God,
you have formed the wild and the wonderful,
the extraordinary and the quirky,
sometimes hidden deep in forests and oceans.
Creator God, we bring our praise.

Creator God,
you have given us fragrance, sight and sound
to enchant and to enthral;
the scent of flowers, the daily newness of sunset
and the trill of birdsong.
Creator God, we bring our praise.

Creator God, for the small detail of delights:
the lark ascending,
stones plopping in water,
rainfall pattering and snowflakes' complex structures.
Creator God, we bring our praise.

Creator God,
you have placed us in your world
as stewards who tend and care for it.
Creator God, make us wise guardians of your world.

Creator God,
you have given us skills to study your world,
to grasp its immensity
and understand its structures.
Creator God, make us wise guardians of your world.

Creator God,
you have given us joy in being active in your world,
in mountaineering, fishing and walking,
playing and gardening.
Creator God, make us wise guardians of your world.

Creator God,
your world has inspired art and music,
drawn out of us our own creativity.
Creator God, make us wise guardians of your world.

Creator God,
for the wonders and the demands of your world
we praise you and we bless you.
Creator God, make us wise guardians of your world.

Creator God,
Father, Son and Holy Spirit,
we praise and bless you
for the privilege and joy of living in your world. *Amen.*

THE CHURCH

The local church

345. The local church

Lord, reveal your glory in and through this church, we pray.
May all people who enter it find a gentle welcome,
may all who touch its walls rest their fingertips on glory,
and may all who sit awhile discover the communion of saints,
may all who sing here find new harmonies and descants to their lives,
and may all who pray here find a thin place
    that invites them to tread on holy ground.
We pray for all who care for this church
and all who love its presence in their midst,
whether they enter it or not.
Bless this church
and make it a blessing to its wider community.
In the name of Jesus Christ we pray. Amen.

346. The local church

Lord of the Church,
may this church be a welcoming place for all who enter its doors,
a spacious place where your light shines,
and all have freedom to explore the questions, joys and sorrows
    that haunt and enhance our daily lives.
Surrounded by strong walls of faith,
held secure by flying buttresses of your presence,
sheltered by the roof of your love
and summoned by the bells of gospel proclamation,
bless us as we steward this church today
for the good of our local community and the glory of your Name. Amen.

347. Cathedrals and churches

Lord God, we thank you for this *cathedral / church*,

for the testimony it bears to your faithfulness over the years,

for the salvation it proclaims and the stories its walls could tell,

for the memories it holds in people's hearts,

and for its place in the local community.

As we worship here today,

following in the footsteps of the saints of the past,

stir us to bolder faith for the future,

expressed in graceful, joyous living.

Accept our liturgy,

our work of love, which we, your people,

offer together in this holy place.

We pray this in the name of Jesus Christ our Lord. Amen.

348. Historic cathedrals and churches

We thank you, Father, for this *cathedral / church*,

whose stones have echoed with centuries of prayer,

in times of joy and in times of fear.

May we, who follow in the footsteps of so many prayerful people,

be ourselves people whose lives are marked

by joyful trust in your goodness

and confident hope in your promises.

We join our prayers with those of all who have visited here today:

those whose prayers were confident and articulate,

those whose prayers were tentative and faltering,

those whose prayers were tears or laughter.

Thank you, Lord, that you have heard them all.

Accept our prayers for the sake of your Son, Jesus Christ our Lord. Amen.

349. Church buildings

For our church buildings, we give you thanks, Lord God;
for the testimony they bear in their stones, glass and tiles
to your faithfulness through the ages,
and the vision of those who built them.
May they continue to sing out their praises to you,
to echo your faithfulness in human hosannas
and by joining the angels in singing "Holy, holy, holy, Lord". Amen.

350. Silence and church buildings

For the gift of buildings in which to worship you,
we thank you, O Lord.
Teach us the many moods and shades of the accumulated silence
    they have enclosed through the ages:
the rich silences of anticipation
and the quiet silences of faithful waiting,
the spacious silences of hope
and the enfolding silences of compassion,
the fearful silences of uncertainty or dread
and the echoing silences of worship.
Teach us to listen to our own silences,
and slow us down to hear the sound of sheer silence
    in this familiar place.
We pray in the name of Jesus Christ our Lord. Amen.

351. The ministry of the local church

Thrill us, O Lord we pray, with the signs of your life in our midst
as we serve you in the community in which you have placed us.
Make this church a locus of rich blessing for all who walk past its doors,
a place of hope for people who are in thrall to despair or distress,
a place of solace for people who are overwhelmed
by a weight of sorrow or sadness that is too much for them to bear,
and a place of astonishing joy for all who dare to seek you here.
We pray in the name of Jesus Christ, our Lord. Amen.

352. The church community

Lord Jesus, you came to build a community
that reflects and embodies the love of God, Father, Son and Holy Spirit.
Draw us more deeply, we pray, into that love with you
and with one another in the community of faith.
We pray that the witness of the church will be faithful to your love,
expressive of your care,
and transformative for the people in our communities.
We ask this in your name, Lord Jesus our Lord. Amen.

353. Unity in the community

Merciful God,
we pray that we may be empowered to live as faithful disciples,
reflecting your goodness in our world.
Enable us to live in unity of spirit
where there is temptation to discord;
with sympathy and love
where there is temptation
to assert ourselves at the expense of the wellbeing of others;
with tender hearts
where it is easier to ride roughshod
or to close our hearts to the inconvenient or the demanding;
and with humble minds
where we are tempted to believe that our opinion is right.
We pray this so that the world may come to know the love of God
made present in our human community. Amen.

354. Our common life

Gracious God,
weave into our common life your gentle mercy and loving kindness,
so that the texture of our being and the manner of our living
may resonate with your courteous presence among us.
Help us to bring consolation and joy to the community
in which you place us.
We pray this in the name of Jesus Christ. Amen.

355. Community

God of community, as you draw us closer,
we find that we are also being drawn closer to other people,
sometimes the most unexpected people.
Then, like a quilter, you create a pattern from our lives,
    joining and binding us together in creative beauty.
Thank you for the people we never expected would be part of our lives
but whose presence we have come to value.
We pray that you will continue to build
vibrant, strong and wonderful communities
that together bear with joy the name, "the body of Christ".
We pray in the name of Jesus Christ. Amen.

356. Saying goodbye to community members

As the time comes to say goodbye,
we pray for . . . as *he / she / they* leave(s) our church community
to follow your calling in a new way.
We thank you for the times we have shared together
and *his / her / their* contribution to our common life,
for the memories we have made,
the challenges we have faced
and the blessings we have known.
Go before *him / her / them* as *he / she / they* leave(s) us.
Give *him / her / them* a smooth transition
and the joy and support of new friends and colleagues,
and continue to bless *his / her / their* ministry
    in the days and years to come.
We pray in the name of Jesus Christ our Lord. Amen.

357. Service

Deliver us, O God,

from misconstrued piety

which cares more for the impression we give

than for true holiness of life.

Fan into flame within us a passion to serve

the people we meet whose needs disturb or haunt us.

Give us an instinctive desire to live with grace and kindness

as salt and light among them.

We pray in the name of Jesus Christ our Lord. Amen.

358. Responding faithfully

When we are perplexed, help us, O Lord,

to move beyond the obvious to discern,

instead, the sometimes astonishing

   and unimaginable ways of responding

which only you can lay before us.

Free us from blinkered vision, preconceived ideas

and tired ways of living and making decisions,

so that we have the courage to live prophetically

in a world that is so often trapped by its own narrow ways of working.

We pray this in the name of Jesus Christ. Amen.

359. Sunday Schools and youth groups

We give thanks, O God,

for the work of Sunday Schools and Christian youth groups.

We pray for the children who are reached by these groups,

all the people who lead or support them,

and the churches which seek to proclaim the good news

   to the younger generation in our community.

Inspire them with vision and creativity.

Bless their work, so that it bears fruit in the transformation of young lives,

and in the formation of young people who are on fire with love for you.

We pray this in the name of Jesus Christ,

who welcomed children into his presence. Amen.

360. The scriptures

Guide us, O Lord,

in our reading, hearing and study of your holy word,

so that we will grow in the knowledge and love of you,

our Creator and Redeemer.

We pray for all people who translate, publish and distribute the scriptures,

and for people who are encountering

    the good news of the gospel for the first time.

In the name of Jesus Christ, our Lord. Amen.

Vocations in the Church

361. Vocations

Lord Jesus Christ,

your call to your disciples transformed their lives

and expanded their vision of what they could become

    when they were led by the Holy Spirit

to step out beyond the boundaries of the familiar into new adventures

as messengers of your gospel.

We pray for people who, today, are being called by you

    to new, perhaps undreamed of, vocations.

Give them attentiveness to the Spirit's nudges,

wise counsellors as they explore their thoughts and feelings,

and delight in responding to your call.

We pray this in your name. Amen.

362. Church leaders

Lord of the Church,
endow the people you have called to leadership with wisdom and vision.
Enable them to give your Church across the world
a joyful example and inspired counsel
for the challenges and opportunities ahead,
so that, together, we may serve you with gladness and delight.
We pray this in the name of Jesus Christ our Lord. Amen.

363. Church leaders*

Lord Jesus, we pray for people called to leadership in your Church.
Make them wise in their thinking and trustworthy in their acting,
careful in their silences and useful in their utterances.
We pray this in your name, O Lord. Amen.

364. New ministry

We pray, O Lord our God,
for . . . as *he / she* takes up a new role in this community of faith,
and we ask for all the needful gifts to fulfil the vocation
   that you are opening up among us.
May the years ahead be times of joy and discovery
as together we walk with you in faith and trust.
Bless this church through *N's* presence among us
and make us, together, a source of hope and strength
   for the wider community we are called to serve.
We pray in the name of Jesus Christ our Lord. Amen.

---

*   Based on the writings of Gregory the Great

365. Leadership in the local church

We pray for the people called to leadership in this church,
for the clergy, *Readers, church workers, churchwardens* and *the PCC,*
and all who volunteer their time and skills.
As we pray for the mission and ministry of this church,
we ask that our common life will be well-ordered
for the good of the local community,
among whom we are set as salt and light,
bearing witness to our Lord Jesus Christ
in whose name we pray. Amen.

366. Deacons

We pray, Lord God, for the people you call
   to serve you as deacons in your church.
We pray for those exploring their vocation or in training,
the people who will be ordained on . . . ,
and the deacons who serve you in churches and communities
   around the world.
As they follow your example of loving service,
venturing into the forgotten corners of the world
as your ambassadors to proclaim the gospel and care for your people,
make them prisms of your pure love,
reflecting it in glorious hues in your world today.
We pray this in the name of Jesus Christ our Lord. Amen.

367. Priests

We pray, O Lord, for all priests in your church,
in their leadership, nurture and care of your people
within and beyond the church doors.
Give them wisdom and insight
into the needs and opportunities they encounter,
bring good fruit from their study, preaching and teaching,
guide them in their oversight of the churches they serve,
and make their pastoral care a blessing to the people
    who look to them to embody
    your loving, hope-filled presence in their midst.
We pray this for the sake of Jesus Christ our Lord. Amen.

368. Bishops

O Lord, our Good Shepherd,
we pray for our bishops whom you have called
to oversight and leadership in your church,
especially N at the beginning of a new phase of ministry.
Give them wisdom and sound judgement,
vision and imagination,
and make them strong and compassionate leaders of your people
in their various callings and ministries,
so that the good news of Jesus Christ may reach
    to the forgotten corners of our society and world.
We pray this in the name of Jesus Christ. Amen.

369. Monastic life

Lord Jesus Christ, we give thanks and pray for all men and women
whom you call to the spacious discipline of life
    in a Religious Order or Community.
May they run in the paths of your commandments,
their hearts overflowing with the inexpressible delights of love.*
May their times of prayer and silence be times of dancing with you,
their times of work bear fruit within and beyond their doors
    and their times of recreation be joyful and creative.
Bless those people who are exploring their vocation to monastic life,
those whose patterned daily life is variously both duty and delight,
and those who face death as the bringing to perfection*
    of their dedication to you alone.
We pray this in your name, O holy Lord. Amen.

370. Team ministry

Lord Jesus, your unusual choice of close disciples,
with their strong and divergent characters and backgrounds,
led to times of tension alongside the joys of friendship.
In that light we pray for the varied people
    in the teams in which we serve,
thanking you for the unique and wonderful gifts and graces
    each one brings.
Help us to value each other,
to enjoy each other's company,
however easy or difficult we may find each other at times;
and to value all the contributions we make to the life
    and ministry of the churches we serve.
In your name we pray, Lord Jesus. Amen.

---

*   *Rule of St Benedict*, Prologue 49, 4

371. Pastoral ministry

Lord Jesus Christ, the Good Shepherd of the sheep,
you listened to the spoken and unspoken needs of people you met
and, with few words, offered new perspectives
    and opened new beginnings.
We pray for all people who offer their listening skills
in the service of people
who yearn to be heard and understood in their need.
Deepen their pastoral insight
and give them the wisdom to know when to keep silence
    and when and how to speak.
Make them channels of your peace, we pray. Amen.

372. Using our particular gifts

O Lord, as we recall the promises made at our baptism
and the empowering of the Holy Spirit at our confirmation,
we know that you have called us each by name
and placed us in the body of Christ
to love and serve you all our lives.
Reveal to us the gifts with which you have endowed us,
and show us the tasks only we can do for you,
because of who we are and where we are placed.
Then, Holy Spirit, send us out in mission,
to use our particular gifts as individuals
and as your local church to proclaim the love of God.
In the name of Jesus Christ our Lord. Amen.

Discipleship and mission

373. The call of Jesus
Lord Jesus, your call comes to us insistently
to follow you and, like your first disciples,
to leave security behind
and go where you lead us.
As we explore the depth and height of your love which holds us fast,
we offer ourselves afresh to love and serve,
trusting that your strength will be made perfect in our weakness,
and that your grace will shine through our lives,
so that the world may see and know
God's love made tangible in its midst.
In your name we pray. Amen.

374. Following Jesus
Lord Jesus, whose friends never guessed
    the impact of your call to follow you:
give us the adventurous spirit and daring trust
    to face the challenges you put before us,
and to live our lives trusting that your burning, searing word
    will transform not only our lives but the life of the world;
keep us, your church, faithful to our calling to follow you,
to be salt and light in the world
and bearers of resurrection hope.
We pray this in your name. Amen.

375. God's call

When your call to us catches us by surprise,
help us, O Lord, to give a steady answer.
When your call feels like an invasion of our space,
help us, O Lord, to move beyond our fears.
When your call is something we cling to and weigh up,
stop us playing for time.
Instead, draw us with your magnetic love
into the mutual dance of a joyful and obedient "Yes".
In the name of Jesus Christ our Lord we pray. Amen.

376. Vocation and commitment

Keep us faithful to our various callings, O Lord.
When the path seems clear and walking it is a joy,
help us to walk steadily and prevent us over-reaching ourselves;
when there seem to be more questions than answers,
give us clarity of thought and focus in our response;
when our faithfulness seems unappreciated
or monotony and repetition wear us down,
give us the stubborn strength to remain faithful to our commitments
and, when difficulties and demands sap our energy,
refresh us and encourage us to keep going.
Wherever you call us to serve you and your people,
may we shine as lights that bring light and life to others.
We pray in your name, Lord Jesus. Amen.

377. Saying "Yes" to God

Help us, Lord Jesus, to say our "Yes" to you,
as your mother did when she abandoned herself to God's love,
saying, "Let it be" to the mystery of God's ways.
Then strengthen us, O Lord,
to remain faithful,
and to repeat that "Yes" through the times of testing,
until new songs of joy burst out in our *Magnificat* to you. Amen.

378. The call of God

When you call us, O God,

give us the courage to take up our cross and follow you,

leaving behind old securities and knowing ourselves held fast by your hand.

Lead us into new explorations of the depth and height

    of your love for us,

and into new expressions of that love in the world around us.

As we go together as your people,

may we prove your strength in our weakness

when we dare to love and serve in your name.

We pray this in the name of Jesus Christ our Lord. Amen.

379. Vocation and pilgrimage

Help us, our Lord,

to recognize your calling as our vocation.

Make us aware of new perspectives to embrace

as we hear and heed your call,

new landscapes that you open up before us,

new joys and new challenges that you throw into our path.

Keep us walking, O pied-piper God,

on the pilgrimage

that you yearn to make of our journey through life,

and lead us into the unknown

with the confidence that we walk with you.

We pray in the name of Jesus Christ,

who walked alongside his friends. Amen.

380. God's coming to us

Whatever messenger you send—
abrupt, loud, majestic, or reticent with solemn, unspoken words
that are understood as much as heard—
prepare us, O Lord,
to welcome your coming among us in fresh and fertile ways.
Make our homes, like Mary's, into places where heaven touches earth,
and where we find that we are wondering at the wonder of your grace.
Amen.

381. Daring mission

Lord, you call us, as you did your disciples,
to follow you and become fishers for people,
bringing the good news of your life and love.
Rather than paddling in the shallows,
observing the little fish we might expect to catch,
give us their daring to throw our nets into the deeps,
where we can neither see what might enter them
nor anticipate what a glorious melee of people
you are drawing to yourself through our obedience.
Teach us to be bold in our discipleship and adventurous in our fishing.
For your sake we make this prayer, Lord Jesus. Amen.

382. Commitment to service

To you, O Lord, we bring our songs of joy.
As we join creation's song of praise,
we lift our hearts in celebration of your great love
and sing with all the choirs of heaven, "Holy, holy, holy Lord".
Refresh our memories of your past goodness;
renew our resolution to serve you in the present;
and stretch our faith in your purposes in the future.
Then send us out to love and serve you
and the people you bring into our lives
with vivacity and with verve, now and always. Amen.

383. Commitment to discipleship

Lord Jesus,
who called your disciples to be with you
and then to go and preach the gospel,
revive our enthusiasm and commitment
to follow in their footsteps
in the world in which you place us today.
We pray this in your name. Amen.

384. Following Jesus

Lord Jesus,
you laid aside your rightful reputation and your glory
to be a servant,
laying aside your garments
and washing the feet of your friends:
show us, by your example
of sharing the life of people who were outcasts,
what it means for us to follow you
    in your paths of humble, costly service.
Draw us with your love and transform us
as you teach us to love, to serve, to follow you alone. Amen.

385. Walking with God

Holy God, you call us to walk to a different drumbeat
    from that of the world around us.
Give us the attentiveness to keep in step with you
    as you lead us through our daily life,
so that, fully alive to your Holy Spirit's guidance,
we may draw others to walk with us
and thus with you, our Lord.
We pray in the name of Jesus Christ. Amen.

386. Walking with Jesus

Lord Jesus, we hear your call to come to you and walk with you,
and we see your scarred hands outstretched to hold ours in safety.
Lead us along life's highways and byways,
and help us to keep in step with you,
trusting your love for us.
In your name we pray. Amen.

387. Life's pilgrimage

Lord Jesus,
keep us in step with your pace on our pilgrim journey,
walking in time with you through the joys that thrill us,
the sorrows that pain us,
and the insights that elude us.
Free those areas of our lives that we have
    barricaded against your kindly mercy,
and enable us to accept the grace that is offered
    through the ordinary things of life.
We pray this in your name. Amen.

388. Living faithfully

Holy God, may our lives,
not just our mouths,
speak of your gracious love
and shine with your holiness in our world today. Amen.

389. Benedictine living

Lead us, Lord God,
in obedience to you
into the paths of stability and conversion of life,
so that our lives,
individually and as a community,
bear witness to the faith that we profess.
We pray in the name of Jesus Christ our Lord. Amen.

390. Stability in life

Just as unknown people built the flying buttresses in a church,
concealed but vital to its enduring strength through the ages,
so, Lord, help us to be patient in building and reinforcing
    the structures needed for our stability in life.
Forgive us when we devote more time to our public image
    than with who we are when naked before you,
and when we do not have time for the hidden work
    that moulds and determines the effectiveness
of our engagement in your world.
Teach us the necessary patience for the long haul
of being your faithful disciples.
We pray in the name of Jesus Christ. Amen.

391. Formation by God—lessons from stonemasons

Stun us, Lord God, with insights into the determination
    behind the building of a stone wall or sculpture.
We thank you for stonemasons whose vision and skill
enable them to see beyond a lump of stone
and to bring to visible form what lies unseen within it.
Enlarge our vision and our patience
to work with you as you chip away, bit by bit,
the things in our own lives that need to go
if you are gradually to bring to life the riches you see hidden in us.
We pray in the name of Jesus Christ,
who continues to build his Church. Amen.

392. The song of angels in our lives

Open our ears, O Lord, to the unexpected song of angels
    singing of your glory in the concert halls of our lives.
Then send us out, like the shepherds,
with the news of your joy, great joy,
revealed in the streets and alleys of our neighbourhoods.
But teach us too, O Lord, what it is to be faithful
    when the angels don't appear to be singing.
We pray this in the name of Jesus Christ our Lord. Amen.

393. Contemplation

Forgive us, Lord, when, in our greed for instant inspiration,
like voyeurs we glance at the scene and miss the picture.
Slow us down, focus our attention,
lead us into contemplation which can unlock new depths
and make us receptive to new gifts.
This we pray in the name of Jesus Christ,
who gave time to consider the lilies of the field. Amen.

394. Retreats and retreat houses

Sing to us, dear Lord, through the elected silence* of a retreat.
Draw us close to you and sing
through the beauty of creation,
through the rhythm of worship,
through the opening of your word,
and through the care of people you call to the ministry of retreats.
We pray for all retreat houses and for all people who live or visit there.
Sing to us, dear Lord, through the elected silence of retreats. Amen.

---

*   Inspired by G. M. Hopkins' poem "Elected silence, sing to me"

395. Spiritual directors and guides

Lord Jesus Christ, when people came to you,
you saw deep into their hearts and lives,
asked them what they wanted,
and spoke few but perceptive words in reply.
We thank you for people you have called to serve you
   as spiritual directors and companions.
Give them acute hearing to detect the unspoken word,
wise insight to discern your action in people's lives,
and gentle reticence in speaking.
Bless their ministry for the good of your Church.
We pray in your name. Amen.

396. New ways to serve God in the world

When you call us, O God,
to step beyond the door of our familiar world of home and work
to explore with vivacity and joy new ways of serving you
and new callings beyond our imagination,
expand our vision and tease out of us new responses of love.
We pray this in our desire that the world may see and rejoice
in the salvation that you alone can give.
In the name of Jesus Christ our Lord. Amen.

397. Mission in the local community

Lord of the Church,
you send us out as ministers of your grace
   into the loveless and hurting *parish / neighbourhood*.
Fill us afresh with compassion for your people,
zest to proclaim the good news,
a keen eye for signs of your presence,
and infectious joy in the life you give us.
Make us trustworthy witnesses to our Lord Jesus Christ. Amen.

398. Missionaries

Lord Jesus Christ,
you sent some people back home to tell what you had done for them,
and others to the ends of the earth to proclaim the good news
in unfamiliar places and cultures.
We pray for all people you send today to places
far from their families and friends:
where the unfamiliar is hard to bear, comfort them,
where it is exhilarating, refresh them with your joy,
where it is dangerous, protect them,
and where it is exhausting, renew and strengthen them.
Bless them and the people they serve in rich and wonderful ways.
We pray this in your name, Lord Jesus. Amen.

399. People finding their way to faith

We pray, Lord God,
for people around us whose faith is as yet inchoate.
Draw them closer to you
and provide for them companions who can help them
to grow in insight and trust in your loving purposes.
Surprise them with glimmerings of joy in the midst of daily routines;
give them clarity of perception as they explore their questions,
and exhilaration in the quest to know and be known by you,
    holy, gracious God. Amen.

400. God's dynamic life

Forgive us, O God,
when our concept of you is too static
    to grasp the potential of your dynamic life;
when our trust in you is too fearful to embrace
any expectation of new hope and direction;
when our love for you is too jaded
to dare to believe that you might yet astound us
with the tenderness and exhilaration of transformative love.
O loving Lord, open our hearts and lives to your presence,
    and free us to respond to you with daring and delight.
We pray this in the name of Jesus Christ,
who revealed your life in the midst of human life. Amen.

401. Christian unity

Lord, you call your Church to a life of holiness,
to bear your beauty in the world
and to display your glorious love for the world
    you created and redeemed:
[in this Week of Prayer for Christian Unity]
forgive our divisions and dissensions,
our listlessness and our laziness.
Transform our meagre love with love divine.
Holy Spirit, come among us, and disturb us
into renewed passion and zest for the good news of the gospel.
We pray this for the glory of Jesus Christ,
the Lord of the Church. Amen.

Baptism, marriage and funerals

402. The birth or baptism of a child
We give you thanks, O God, for the *birth / baptism* of . . . .
As *he / she* joins our community of faith,
pour your blessing on *him / her* and *his /her* family
and grant us all the joy of seeing *his / her* growth in life and faith.
We pray in the name of Jesus Christ our Lord. Amen.

403. Baptism of an adult or child
Lord Jesus, you call us by name;
in you we are adopted and made members of your family:
we pray for *(N) / those* to be baptized *today / in this church / this Easter*.
We pray that as *he / she / they is / are* signed with the cross,
your call on their lives will meet a ready response
and *he / she / they* will join with your Church
in proclaiming the good news of your gospel,
sharing with us the inheritance of the saints in light.
We ask this in your name, Lord Jesus. Amen.

404. Baptism of a baby or child
Bless, O Lord, *N,* who we baptize and welcome into your Church.
Grant *him / her* healthy development,
an inquiring mind to explore the wonder of your world,
and an open, grateful heart ready to trust in you
as *he / she* grows in knowledge of your love.
We pray for *his / her* parents and godparents *(NN . . .)*
as they take on the responsibility of raising this child
to know and love God and neighbour,
and for the wider family as they support them in this lively endeavour.
We pray this in the name of Jesus Christ our Lord. Amen.

405. Marriage

God of boundless love,
we praise you that you have led *N and N*
   to make their public commitment to each other.
Bless them in their marriage;
daily teach them how to give and receive care,
to laugh together and to forgive when the need arises.
Permeate their lives and home with peace
and grant them strength for the years ahead,
so that their marriage may become a blessing
to all who will share their circle of friendship.
We pray this in the name of Jesus Christ,
who enjoyed a wedding celebration with family and friends. Amen.

406. Recent or future marriage

God of boundless love,
we praise you for *N and N*
who *were / will be* married in this church.
Bless them in their life together,
and bless their families and friends
who *gathered / will gather* to celebrate with them.
May their marriage grow in depth of love
and become a source of life and joy
to all who will share their circle of friendship.
We pray this in the name of Jesus Christ,
who enjoyed a wedding celebration with family and friends. Amen.

407. Renewal of marriage vows

We thank you, O loving God, for *N and N*
who have shared mutual love in the years of their marriage
and rejoice with them for your many blessings.
We pray for them today
as they renew the vows they made on the threshold of their life together,
and ask that the years to come, however few or many,
will be times of deepening love and growing appreciation
    of the gifts and challenges of more mature love.
Bless them *(and their family)* as they turn afresh to you.
We pray this in the name of Jesus Christ our Lord. Amen.

408. Bereavement

Lord Jesus, you knew the love of family and friends
    and wept at the tomb of your friend Lazarus.
Comfort us as we gather to make our farewells to *N*
whose life among us has enriched us and whose death leaves us bereft.
In our mourning, turn our eyes to you,
and open our ears to hear your words of comfort and hope
that you will never leave us or forsake us.
Give us daily strength for the path ahead,
and as we begin this next stage of life on earth,
we entrust *N* to *his / her* new life in your presence.
Be with us day by day, dear Lord, we pray. Amen.

409. Bereavement (including difficult memories)
As we remember N,
we bring our thanks for all that *he / she* has meant to us:
for the goodness and kindness we experienced from *him / her*
and the memories we will cherish.
As we remember that no one is perfect,
we pray for people with more difficult memories
and ask for their healing and peace now that N has died.
May your love surround us
as we begin a new phase of life without N among us.
Help us to grieve well and rebuild our lives
that have been diminished by bereavement,
so that our future may be testimony to N's ongoing legacy for good.
We pray this, gracious Lord Jesus, in your name. Amen.

410. People who mourn
O Lord of life who conquered death,
you bore our sorrows on the cross
and knew the pain of losing loved ones:
we pray that you will console and comfort
those who mourn *(the death of . . .)*.
Remind us afresh of the sure and certain hope
    of the resurrection of the dead,
so that, despite our grief, we may sing a confident "Alleluia" to you,
who turns death into the gateway to life eternal. Amen.

411. People who mourn
Comfort all who mourn, O Lord, we pray.
Surround them with tenderness at their time of loss.
Inspire them with hope amidst the sadness,
and, in due time, turn their mourning into dancing.
We pray this in the name of Jesus Christ our Lord. Amen.

SAINTS AND SEASONS

412. The Church year

"Jesus must get really bored. He is born and dies every year."*
Lord Jesus, thank you for the joy of Christmas celebrations
and every year's fresh wonder at your incarnation.
Thank you for the solemnity of Holy Week
and its sobering reminder of the cost of our salvation.
Thank you for the extraordinariness of Easter
and the joy that bursts into our lives with your resurrection.
Thank you for never being bored with sharing your life with us. Amen.

Advent

413. Advent litany

Come among us, Lord.
Come, Lord Jesus.
God of the Advent season,
your silence sometimes feels like absence,
yet your presence is overwhelming:
come among us to save us,
and disturb us with your hope.
Make of us a people who prepare your way
that all may rejoice in your salvation.
Come among us, Lord.
Come, Lord Jesus.

---

*   *a six-year-old member of Durham Cathedral Sunday School*

God of the Advent season,
your hope is tangible and captivating,
your promise is sure and will be fulfilled:
come to us in our confusion and our need
and disturb us with your justice;
Make of us a people who will not be satisfied
until your kingdom comes.
Come among us, Lord.
Come, Lord Jesus.

God of the Advent season,
your justice is expansive in its scope,
and relentless in its probing of our ways:
come to your world in its cruelty and its agony
and disturb us with your comfort;
make of us a people who will not falter
in our compassion and our care.
Come among us, Lord.
Come, Lord Jesus.

God of the Advent season,
your compassion is unbounded
and your ways beyond our understanding:
come to your world in its noise and in its tears,
and disturb us with your silence;
make of us a people by whose peace
thousands around us may come to salvation.
Come among us, Lord.
Come, Lord Jesus.

414. Disturbance and hope
Disturbing God,
whose Advent shakes the old foundations of the earth,
shine your light in the darkness of this world's suffering,
that in places of injustice and oppression
your dawn will break with new life and hope,
brought to us through Jesus Christ our Lord,
in whose name we pray. Amen.

415. Wake up
God, our Father,
wake us up to see your light breaking in your world;
wake us up to hear the promise that our redemption is drawing near;
wake us up to take seriously your coming judgement;
wake us up to the promise that Christ will come again in glory
and bids us all be ready for the dawning of that glorious day.
This Advent wake us up, O Lord, we pray. Amen.

416. Advent expectation
Lord Jesus Christ,
your Advent shakes the world to its core:
shake our souls with expectation and fear,
enchant us with joy and wonder
and invite us to live with new hope through your coming amongst us.
In your name we pray. Amen.

417. Advent amidst the winter scenery
When roaring winds churn up the russet carpet of residual autumn
and ballerinas of spray cascade over rocky coasts
when summer's long light yields to winter's long night,
and all is wild and wonderful,
then, O Lord, reach into the windswept places of our hearts
and sing to us through the poetry of your world
that Advent hope is true, is true. Amen.

418. Openness to God

Holy God, as once you came to Mary in the midst of her daily life,
so, we pray, come to us this week in new and wondrous ways.
Give us the courage and the joy to pray, as she did:
"Let it be with me according to your word." Amen.

419. People in need as Christmas approaches

As Christmas approaches, we pray, gracious Lord,
for all for whom this will not be a joyful time,
for all who are sick, suffering or bereaved,
and all who work to care for them, *(especially . . . ,)*
for all who are unemployed or not earning enough to make ends meet,
for parents who cannot give their children
     the Christmas celebration of their dreams,
for all who are isolated and have no one to share Christmas with,
and whose memories haunt them,
and for all who are homeless or whose homes are dangerous places to be.
Lord Jesus, draw near to them,
and stir us into action in situations where we can be
     your presence to people in need.
In your name we pray. Amen.

Christmas

420. Open to God

Open our ears, O Lord, to hear the song of angels singing your glory
and, like the shepherds, to rush to respond.
Open our eyes, O Lord, to see your majesty revealed in a humble place
and to wonder and worship at this miracle.
Open our hands, O Lord, to offer our gifts
and to reach out and care for those in need.
Open our minds, O Lord, to grasp new hints of meaning
    in this strange marvel, so familiar yet so unknown.
And open our hearts to burst with joy and hope,
so that, amidst the tears and trials of our world,
your light may shatter darkness once again.
In your name we pray. Amen.

421. Nativity petitions

Lord Jesus, you were born in a stable:
We pray for all who are homeless and lonely,
Lord Jesus, Mary and Joseph cared for you.
We pray for all who are vulnerable or unloved,
Lord Jesus, angels sang the news of your birth.
We pray for Christians around the world
as they tell others of the good news of Christmas,
Lord Jesus, the shepherds went to Bethlehem to find the Holy Family:
We pray that many will turn and seek you this Christmas.
Lord Jesus, the wise men travelled long distances and brought their gifts:
We pray that you will accept the gifts of love and service that we bring,
Lord Jesus, King Herod's fear at your birth
    led to the suffering of innocent babies and families:
We pray for people whose lives are in danger today
    from corrupt and ruthless leaders,
Lord Jesus, Prince of Peace, we pray that your peace
    will enfold your world this Christmas. Amen.

422. Peace on earth

Lord Jesus, as we, in our imaginations,
quietly enter the stable where you were born,
gather with the shepherds in their worship,
and join the song of the angels, "Glory to God in the highest",
we pray for your peace to come on earth as it is in heaven. Amen.

423. The Naming and Circumcision of Jesus (1 January)

For a baby named "Yahweh, God, is salvation"
we bring our awed gratitude, O Lord.
As Mary and Joseph fulfilled the law
and brought their firstborn son into the covenant people,
so that he, born of woman,
born under the law,
could redeem those who were under the law,
may we be faithful to the holy way of life
to which you call us as your adopted children.
We pray this in the name of Jesus, "God is salvation". Amen.

424. New Year

Gracious God,
at the turn of a new year,
as bells ring out and midnight fireworks are lit,
hopes for a better future are raised and resolutions made,
remind us again of our dependence on you
if aspirations are to be more than regrets this time next year.
As we praise you for blessings in past years,
we pray for peace and prosperity for all people in the coming year,
and entrust our futures into your hands.
Lord, this year, make us instruments of your peace. Amen.

Epiphany

425. Epiphany: revelation of Jesus Christ
Lord Jesus Christ,
your glory was revealed in a family home to wise men come from afar,
and on a mountain to bemused friends who thought they knew you:
reveal yourself to us in the midst of our searching and our living,
not just in the big moments for which we have laboured long,
but also when we are unprepared and bewildered.
Give us the courage to live faithfully
in the light of your presence among us,
so that your glory may be revealed through our living.
We ask this in your name. Amen.

426. Epiphany: holy curiosity
O God, the Father of our Lord Jesus Christ,
your Son was revealed to wise scholars who travelled far
    because of curiosity about the meaning of a star in the sky.
Grant us holy curiosity about the wonders we see in your creation,
so that we, as they did, may change our course to explore your purposes
in the sometimes too-familiar world we see around us.
We pray this in the name of Jesus Christ our Lord. Amen.

427. Epiphany: light shining in the darkness
When light shines in darkness and epiphanies may be at hand,
catch our attention, Lord, and make us light-bearers;
when family celebrations are blessed with your presence,
give us deeper joy in our relationships with those around us;
when obedience to your calling elicits revelations from heaven,
keep us faithful, O Lord, to the implications of your hand on our lives,
and when there are sudden moments of transfigured glory,
stun us into transformed obedience to your Son,
in whose name we pray. Amen.

428. Epiphany: perseverance

Lord, if we read the story carefully, there was nothing very wise
    about the Magi who blundered in going to see King Herod,
yet they had travelled far to explore your purposes and were rewarded
    with the sight of your incarnate Son living quietly in a simple home.
Challenge us by their example to persevere
when we catch a glimpse of something extraordinary,
to seek you amidst the power-play of this world
and not to be ashamed to go to backwaters and humble places
where we might find you dwelling.
Grant this prayer for your glory
and the furtherance of your kingdom here on earth. Amen.

429. The Baptism of Christ (First Sunday of Epiphany)

Lord Jesus, at your baptism you were revealed as Son of God:
we pray for *NN / all those* who are
    preparing for baptism / have been baptized recently;
reveal yourself to them in new and wondrous ways,
and through the empowering of the Holy Spirit
    give them the tenacity and loving commitment
to continue as your disciples until their lives' end.
In your name we pray. Amen.

**430. The Presentation of Christ in the Temple
(Candlemas) (2 February)**

Like Mary and Joseph,
may we offer you, O Lord, our most treasured possessions,
entrusting to you the people we most deeply love.
Like Simeon and Anna,
may we be alert to the unlikely sign of your presence in our midst
and respond with faithful openness and ready wills
to your unexpected ways.
We pray this in the name of our Lord Jesus Christ,
who was presented in the temple. Amen.

Lent and Passiontide

431. Ash Wednesday

As the ashes mark our foreheads for this one day,
mark our lives permanently with the cross of our Lord Jesus Christ:
this Lent may our lives be marked with expressions
of our baptismal commitment to repent and turn from our sins,
to keep a holy Lent and to grow into the likeness of Christ,
who walked the way of the cross
for the sake of the world that he so loved. Amen.

432. The gift of Lent

For Lent's spacious discipline we give you thanks, O Lord:
for the gift of focused time to spring clean our souls,
for the gift of honesty about our wants
that shout in the space created by abstinence,
for the gift of encountering truths drowned out
by the noise of normal life,
for the gift of being refreshed
by ripples of grace in the wilderness,
for the gift of ourselves
as we walk the pilgrim way.
Walk with us, this Lent, O Lord, we pray. Amen.

433. Lent: resisting temptation

Holy Spirit of God,
who drove Jesus into the wilderness to be tempted, as we are,
    yet without succumbing to sin,
lead us daily in the ways of God.
Strengthen us to resist temptation,
and inspire us to turn opportunities for selfishly meeting our own needs
into service to the people for whom our Lord died and was raised,
so that God's kingdom may come on earth as it is in heaven. Amen.

434. Lent: learning obedience

Lord Jesus Christ,
this Lent wean us from our complaints and doubts.
Turn our hearts and wills
to learn obedience
and to walk with joy in your footsteps of fidelity.
We pray this in your name. Amen.

435. The grace of Lent

Lord God of mercy and refreshment,
open our eyes in this grace-filled season of Lent
to see your face amidst the trials and temptations of daily life.
May your Church keep a holy Lent,
that the world may be blessed
as new hope is embodied in its midst.
We ask this in the name of our Lord Jesus Christ,
in whose footsteps we seek to walk. Amen.

436. Walking faithfully in Lent

As we walk the way of Lent,
the way of Jesus Christ who was tempted as we are, yet without sin,
give us the steadfast determination to follow in his footsteps,
the courage to turn for forgiveness when we have sinned,
and the deep desire to be your agents of transformation in the world.
We pray this in his name. Amen.

437. Steadfastness in Passiontide

Lord Jesus Christ,
who, for the joy that was set before you,
endured the cross and its shame,
and, in depths of love beyond our knowledge,
made known to us the love of God.
This Passiontide, give us the grace and steadfastness
to fix our eyes on you,
the pioneer and perfecter of our faith,
and to walk the way of the cross with you.
In your name we pray. Amen.

438. Passiontide: suffering for the gospel

We pray this Passiontide for Christians who suffer
for the sake of the gospel in the world today;
Lord Jesus, strengthen them in their daily living,
give them the courage to remain faithful to their calling,
and for the joy that is set before them,
with you to endure the cross, despising its shame,
keeping their eyes on you, the pioneer and perfecter of their faith.
Bless and comfort them and their families
and make them a blessing to others,
and keep us mindful and prayerful of them this Passiontide,
for your sake and for your glory. Amen.

439. Palm Sunday

"Hosanna, Lord", we cry:
come to our hearts as Lord and king.
"Hosanna, Lord", we cry:
light of the world, shine in the darkness
and disturb in us the empty peace
that has no place for the grief and pain you knew.
"Hosanna, Lord", we cry:
O Prince of Peace,
may our "Hosanna" today
never join the shouting that led you to Calvary,
but be sung with fidelity, come what may.
In your name we pray. Amen.

440. Holy Week

Lord Jesus, as we hear once again the gospel stories
    of your arrest, trial and crucifixion,
open our ears to hear beyond the familiar words.
We give you thanks for your perseverance in the face of cruelty
to save the world that you so loved.
We pray for our world in its ruthlessness to the vulnerable;
its malice when self-interests are threatened,
and its pitilessness when faced with the suffering of the weak and needy.
Cast down those who use their power to abuse others,
and raise up the humble and meek.
We pray for people who respond with compassion, kindness and
    practical help when faced with unimaginable horrors.
Strengthen them in their relief of suffering
and guide us all into a way of living shaped by justice and fairness.
In your name we pray. Amen.

441. Maundy Thursday

Lord Jesus, wash our feet and cleanse our hearts,

that we may be holy in your sight.

Give us the courage never to deny you in front of others,

and feed us with the bread and wine of your life.

As we begin our observance of these holy days,

forgive us when we, like your disciples, fail to keep watch with you

and scatter at the first sign of danger.

Give us the grace to weep at the realization of our sins,

and then to turn to seek your healing.

In your holy name we pray. Amen.

442. Good Friday: the cross

O God, our Father,

this Good Friday, as we contemplate the horror of the cross,

grant us a glimpse of the mystery

that, in Jesus Christ, our God should take human flesh,

and be led to death for sinners' sake.

Then turn our hearts in repentance and hope to you,

our creator and redeemer. Amen.

443. Good Friday: the cries of the world

Holy God, on this Good Friday

we hold before you in silence the clamour of the world:

its cries for justice and peace,

its yearning for health and wholeness,

and its rejection of your way of life and salvation.

Father, into your hands we commend ourselves and our hurting world.

Amen.

444. Good Friday: the peace of Jerusalem
Lord Jesus,
as you wept over Jerusalem,
we grieve with you the continuing violence
of that city and so many cities around the world,
and we pray for their people's peace.
On this most holy of days,
we turn in confident hope that light will shine in the darkness,
that life will conquer death,
and that nations and peoples will be reconciled
by the salvation secured through your death and resurrection.
We pray for the peace of Jerusalem. Amen.

Easter

445. Easter rejoicing
Lord Jesus Christ, we rejoice that you are risen from the dead,
trampling down death by death, and shattering its power to bind.
With your holy Church around the world we sing our Easter "Alleluia"
with hearts and minds renewed and joy unbounded.
Risen Lord, turn the sin and sorrow of this world
to joy and peace in your resurrection life.
In your holy name we pray. Amen.

446. Easter: the empty tomb

Risen Lord, whose disciples could not make sense
    of what they heard that first Easter Day,
open our minds to receive new insights from an empty tomb.
Like Thomas, may our doubts and questions not deter us
from staying with your people until you are revealed to us;
and like Cleopas and his companion, may we be ready to turn around
and run to tell what we have heard and seen.
Risen Lord, in this joyful Eastertide,
transform our ways of living with your resurrection life. Amen.

447. Easter: grief and joy

Lord Jesus, you interrupted mourning and rituals of devotion,
treading instead a new path of joy and resurrection:
like the aghast women at the tomb
may we be ready to let go of our grief
 and follow you as you go before us with resurrection life. Amen.

448. Easter: Jesus the gardener

Lord Jesus,
sometimes, like Mary,
we mistake you for the gardener of an old way of life:
this Eastertime invite us to walk with you
in the garden of your new creation.
O gardener of the world,
may the leaves of the tree of life bring healing to the nations.
Like Mary, call us by name
and send us to be instruments of your peace. Amen.

449. Easter: Jesus and Peter

Lord Jesus, Peter's friend,
what was in your eyes
when you turned and looked at him when he denied you?
Lord Jesus, Peter's friend,
what tone of voice did you use
when you took him aside after that seashore breakfast
and asked him if he loved you?
Lord Jesus, Peter's friend,
what love and trust filled your heart
when you turned your fallible friend's life upside down
and sent him to feed your sheep?
Lord Jesus, Peter's friend,
you call us friends.
Help us to hold your gaze, to hear your hard questions
and to go wherever you send us. Amen.

450. The unexpectedness of resurrection

When we anticipate a closed tomb
   and instead are confronted with emptiness,
challenged by strangers to see beyond what we expected,
and faced with the dismantling of our points of reference,
give us the courage not to be afraid
but, like the women at the tomb,
to dare to speak what we have seen
and to bear witness to resurrection hope. Amen.

451. The Emmaus Road

Risen Lord Jesus,
as you opened the eyes of the people on the Emmaus Road
and stirred their hearts,
speak your word today to our slow and doubting hearts,
then send us, like them, fired with joy
to spread the good news of your resurrection. Amen.

452. Ascension Day

Holy God,

you raised your Son, our Lord Jesus Christ, from the dead,

and exalted him to your right hand in glory:

raise our sights and our hearts to heaven

but keep our feet firmly on the ground,

and send us, like those first disciples,

to bear witness to his ascension in the world he shared with us.

In his name we pray. Amen.

453. Ascension and wounds

Lord Jesus, you took your wounds into heaven

and assure us there is a place in heaven for our wounds

    that we bear in our hearts and in our bodies:

with the first disciples we worship you

and pray that you will empower us afresh, like them,

to bear witness to your glory in this wounded world.

In your name we pray. Amen.

454. Pentecost: the coming of the Holy Spirit

Holy Spirit, come among us

come in gentleness and love,

come as rushing wind and tongues of flame,

come as Advocate, with us for ever.

Fill our hearts and burn within us,

redirect our gaze when it wanders

until our eyes are fixed on Jesus

and our lives reflect God's grace. Amen.

455. Pentecost: the Spirit of transformation

Holy Spirit, God of Pentecostal transformation,
come afresh to your Church to renew us and sanctify us for service.
Turf us out of complacency into action,
out of short-sightedness into clarity of vision,
out of fear for our reputation into fearlessness
    to proclaim the gospel news,
and out of mundaneness and routine
into passion to see God's kingdom come on earth as it is in heaven.
Holy Spirit, breathe into and through our lives,
and reveal the glory of God in our corners of the world. Amen.

Other festivals

456. The Annunciation of our Lord to the Blessed Virgin Mary (25 March)

Gracious God,
on this day we give thanks for Mary's feisty obedience
    to your call on her life,
    and her lifelong fidelity to walk on your unfolding path.
When we are perplexed by your ways in our lives,
stunned by the import of your call on our lives,
and bemused by how all this can be in our lives,
remind us afresh of Mary's courage and commitment.
Give us the grace and gumption to follow her example
of saying "Yes! Yes, let this be with me according to your will."
We pray this in the name of Jesus Christ, her son, our Lord. Amen.

457. The Annunciation in lives today (25 March)

We pray, today, Lord
for all who are quietly faithful to you in their everyday lives
and then suddenly find themselves caught up, by you,
in events beyond their comprehension.
Like Mary, when Gabriel visited her,
may they have the wit to ask questions,
patience to listen for the answer
and grace to walk with you through whatever you call them to.
We pray this in the name of Jesus Christ our Lord,
whose mother set him an example of faithful obedience to you. Amen.

458. Annunciation: God's intervention in our lives (25 March)

As we remember Mary's encounter with Gabriel,
so unexpected and so transformative,
keep us open, O Lord, to your sudden intervention
 in the direction our lives are taking
and help us to respond as faithfully as she did.
In the name of Jesus Christ, her son, we pray. Amen.

459. The Transfiguration of our Lord (6 August)

Holy God, your radiant and resplendent light
 shone in the face of Jesus Christ:
shine your light in our lives today,
disturb our complacency,
and expand our hope,
that we may be faithful to our calling
to be your disciples and live as light in the world.
We pray this in the name of Jesus Christ our Lord. Amen.

460. Holy Cross Day (14 September)

Lord, you made an instrument of shameful death
   to be the means of life and salvation
when our Lord Jesus humbled himself
and became obedient to death, even death on a cross:
as we rejoice in the salvation secured
through his dying and rising again,
keep us faithful to the sign of the cross
made on our foreheads at baptism,
so that we never boast in anything
   except the cross of Jesus Christ our Lord,
in whose holy name we pray. Amen.

461. All Saints' Day (1 November)

Stir us, O Lord, through the stories of your saints,
to deeper love, greater faith and bolder witness.
As we remember them with thanksgiving,
open our eyes to the opportunities to live saintly lives in our world today,
whether in the mundane routines of daily life
or the exposed platforms of the public eye.
Wherever we are called to be, may their example
be an inspiration and a challenge to greater fidelity to you.
In the name of Jesus Christ we pray. Amen.

Saints' Days

462. The variety of saints
O holy and surprising God,
you free us to express our humanity in myriad ways:
we thank you for your saints of years gone by
whose lives inspire us with their faith,
their compassion and their steadfastness.
Help us to thank you too for the saints whose stories disturb us:
those awkward companions who challenge our status quo
or embarrass us with their actions.
As we remember them,
draw us into the great company of all your saints
    to rejoice with them in your salvation,
so that we, like them, may shine with your light in your world.
We pray this in the name of Jesus Christ our Lord. Amen.

463. Saints
For all the saints, we praise your name, O Lord,
not just for the well-known ones
whose examples sometimes seem beyond our reach,
but for the ordinary, the quirky, the unsung and the undervalued,
who were as faithful to you in daily life as the famous saints,
and who shone as lights in the darkness
    of their small corners of your world,
with a loveliness and holiness beyond compare.
Inspire us to follow their example of steadfast,
dogged love and living for your glory.
We pray this in the name of our Lord Jesus Christ,
who enabled his rag-bag of disciples to become saints. Amen.

464. Our forebears in the faith

Thank you, Lord for the enormous variety of ways to serve you,
and for our forebears in the faith who lived faithfully in their day,
especially today for . . .
Excite us by their example and prompt us to follow it
in ways appropriate to our life in your world today.
We pray this in your name, Lord Jesus Christ. Amen.

465. The Week of Prayer for Christian Unity (18–25 January)

As we celebrate the conversion of your servant Paul,
encourage us with the possibilities of miracles beyond our imagination,
so that, like Ananias, whom you called
to go to the persecutor of the Church,
we are prepared to act despite our forebodings
and to step out beyond our comfort zones.
In this Week of Prayer for Christian Unity,
surprise us with your life in unlikely people and places
and send us together, like Paul, to bear witness to your resurrection life.
In your name we pray. Amen.

466. The Conversion of Paul (25 January)

We pray, O God, for people who today,
like Paul before his conversion,
are determined to persecute your Church;
or like Paul after his encounter on the Damascus Road,
find all they once believed turned upside down
and need someone to help them see afresh.
We pray too for all people who, like Paul after his conversion,
are faithful to your new calling
to bear witness to your death and resurrection.
Turn their hearts to you,
and turn our hearts to you,
so that with Paul we may run and finish the race
that you have set before us.
In your name we pray. Amen.

467. Joseph of Nazareth (19 March)

For Joseph, O Lord, we give thanks:
for his faithful action amidst the turmoil of his times,
for his careful response when Mary broke the extraordinary news,
for his trust in your word
    when you revealed to him your strange purposes,
for his prompt action to protect his family in the face of danger,
for his untrumpeted daily care through Jesus's growing years,
for his training of his sons in a useful trade,
and for his example to his family of fidelity to the faith of his ancestors.
We pray for fathers and foster fathers today who, like Joseph,
are faced with more than they anticipated,
and who fear they cannot cope with all the responsibilities laid on them.
Strengthen them for the role to which they are called,
and provide for them the support that they need.
In your name we pray. Amen.

468. George, Martyr (23 April)

In honouring your servant, George,
we pray, O Lord, for the courage to serve you steadfastly
through being faithful in our vocation in life
and unflinching in our trust in you
should that vocation lead to persecution or death.
As we remember George's example,
we pray for people who today are persecuted for their faith
or bribed in an attempt to persuade them to renounce it.
As many nations and cities look to George as their patron,
we pray that his example will permeate their civic lives,
so that not only people but whole communities may live godly lives
and work together to bring holy living to bear on earth.
We pray this in the name of Jesus Christ our Lord. Amen.

469. Mark the Evangelist (25 April)

For faithful Christian mothers and uncles, like St Mark's,
we give you thanks, O Lord;
for opportunities to go on great adventures to proclaim your gospel,
we give you thanks, O Lord;
for mentors, like Paul and Barnabas, when we are young in faith,
we give you thanks, O Lord
for the chance to try again when we, like Mark,
have found the going hard and ducked out of your call,
we give you thanks, O Lord;
and for Mark's vision and commitment
to record eyewitness accounts of our Lord Jesus Christ,
we give you thanks, O Lord.
For St Mark, may your name be praised. Amen.

470. Mark and his Gospel

As we remember Mark and the three other Evangelists,
who took the time to collect and record the stories about Jesus,
we give thanks for the gift of their Gospels
with different perspectives but one common theme:
to bear witness to our Lord Jesus Christ.
Today we thank you for Mark's almost breathless telling
of the story of his Lord.
We pray for people who today
translate these Gospels into new languages
and for people reading or hearing the Gospels for the first time,
that this may be the beginning of the good news of Jesus Christ,
the Son of God, in their lives.
We pray this in the name of Jesus Christ our Lord,
to whom the Gospels bear glorious witness. Amen.

471. Philip and James, Apostles (1 May)

As we celebrate St Philip and St James,
we give you thanks, Lord Jesus, for calling them to be your disciples,
and for their dogged discipleship out of the limelight
but in the crucible of life in the group closest to you.
Recalling Philip's request that you show them the Father
    and James's endurance of being called "the Less",
we pray for people today who find it hard to make sense
    of your presence or feel inferior to others who seem
    to be so much more confident than they are,
people who never do anything spectacular
yet remain faithful plodders for your kingdom.
Thank you for calling them, thank you for calling each of us.
Keep us, like Philip and James, faithful to the ends of our lives. Amen.

472. Matthias the Apostle (14 May)

For St Matthias who faithfully followed Jesus
without being called to be one of the Twelve,
we give thanks and we pray that, like him,
we may be trustworthy when not in the limelight.
We remember his strength of character which led the eleven disciples
to identify him as a candidate to replace Judas,
and pray that our Christian living
    may similarly be honouring to our Lord.
We remember his willingness to face any ambivalence involved
    in replacing a man who had betrayed his Lord,
and pray that we may be faithful to our calling, whatever the cost.
We remember that he faded from public profile
    in the stories of the early Church,
yet may have died as a martyr far from home,
and pray that we, like him, may proclaim the gospel steadfastly.
In the name of Jesus Christ, Matthias's Lord and our Lord. Amen.

473. The Visit of the Blessed Virgin Mary to Elizabeth (31 May)

When we remember the visit of Mary to Elizabeth,
the explosion of joy that it evoked,
and how Elizabeth's unborn child leapt in her womb at Mary's arrival,
we give thanks for friends and family
to whom we can turn when life takes an unplanned turn.
We thank you for Elizabeth's fidelity to you
through her hard decades of childlessness
and for Mary's trust that her elderly, pregnant cousin
     would understand her predicament.
We pray that we, like Elizabeth,
may be gracious to welcome and encourage those who are younger
or facing perplexing situations.
We pray, too, for women who have no one close to them
     to turn to for help and advice with their pregnancies,
for the work of agencies which support women in this situation,
and for children who are born into difficult or
     unsupportive family circumstances.
In the name of Jesus Christ our Lord, we pray. Amen.

474. Barnabas the Apostle (11 June)

For people who, like Barnabas, are "full of the Holy Spirit and of faith"
     we praise you, O God,
for their generosity with their worldly goods we praise you, O God,
for their encouragement of others,
and their willingness to dream unimaginable dreams,
like turning the former persecutor Saul into an apostle of the gospel,
and then to give their lives to be part of
     the experiment of mission that ensued,
we praise you, O God.
May Barnabas, and people like him,
be our example of discipleship today.
We pray in Jesus's holy name. Amen.

475. The Birth of John the Baptist (24 June)

Just as the birth of John brought great joy to his parents
and set in motion his calling to be the forerunner of his cousin, Jesus,
we pray for families welcoming new babies today:
may they offer their joy in thanksgiving to you, O Lord.
We pray for parents like Zechariah and Elizabeth,
who will raise their children perhaps knowing
    they will not live to see them as adults,
      and who balance their own expectations, hopes and dreams
      with the child's freedom to develop in its own way.
We give thanks for the wider families to which we belong,
and on this day, we pray in particular for our cousins,
for their wellbeing and their vocation in life.
In the name of Jesus Christ, John's cousin and our Lord. Amen.

476. Peter and Paul, Apostles (29 June)

Today, Lord Jesus, when we commemorate
Peter, your dear and fallible friend,
and Paul, once the zealous persecutor of your friends,
who were never by nature likely companions,
remind us afresh of the gospel miracle that they are celebrated together.
We thank you for each one's passion to proclaim the gospel
    in the face of persecution and imprisonment,
for their preaching of the gospel to Jewish people and Gentile nations,
for the parts of the New Testament that bear their names
or which they inspired,
and for their faithfulness even to martyrdom for the sake of their Lord.
Inspire us, Lord Jesus, by their examples
as you send us out in your mission today.
In your name we pray. Amen.

477. Peter and Paul: commitment

"Who are you, Lord?" "Who do you say that I am?"
When we hear these questions from the lives of St Peter and St Paul,
challenge us afresh, Lord, in our commitment,
and give us the wisdom, faith and courage
to act on the answer that you are the Messiah,
the Holy One, calling us to your service. Amen.

478. Peter and Paul: people who differ

Lord Jesus, we remember with thanksgiving
    your work in and through St Peter and St Paul,
with their very different backgrounds and educational attainments,
which, at times, led them to divergent perspectives.
We pray for the people from and with whom we differ
    in our sharing of your ministry.
Help us to see the good in them,
to learn from them and to be grateful for them,
as brothers and sisters in the fellowship of the gospel.
We pray this in your holy name. Amen.

479. Thomas the Apostle (3 July)

Lord Jesus, forgive us when we mistake Thomas's caution
    when all was confusion for doubt
and overlook his dogged commitment to go with you to death,
if necessary at Bethany and ultimately in India.
Instead, give us the courage to stay with you as he did,
to ask the obvious questions and wait for answers,
and then to throw caution to the wind to go wherever you send us
with Thomas as our example and inspiration,
confessing, with him, that you are our Lord and our God. Amen.

480. Mary Magdalene (22 July)

Lord Jesus Christ,

gardener of the new creation,

who called Mary Magdalene to step beyond

   the conventions that shaped her life,

and challenge the disbelief of those around her

with the simple yet turbulent words, "I have seen the Lord":

be a gardener in our lives too,

that we may bear the fruit of your Holy Spirit.

In your name we pray. Amen.

481. Mary Magdalene: the example of her response

We pray, O Lord, for people who, as Mary Magdalene once did,

face oppression from forces beyond their control:

bring them to the freedom she came to know.

We pray for people who, as Mary Magdalene once did,

give generously of their financial resources and time

to support the proclamation of the gospel of Jesus Christ:

give them joy in their giving and challenge us to follow their example.

We pray for people who, as Mary Magdalene once did,

stay alongside people who are suffering

   and dying in terrible circumstances:

strengthen their compassion and protect them from recurring trauma.

We pray for people who, as Mary Magdalene once did,

bear witness to the miracle of your resurrection:

empower by your Holy Spirit all who proclaim the good news today,

and give us open ears to hear you call us, too, by name,

and then to go with the good news of what we have seen and heard. Amen.

482. Mary Magdalene: being called by name

Risen Lord Jesus,
when we, like Mary Magdalene at the tomb,
mistake you for someone else
and overlook your presence alongside us,
speak our names and still our hearts,
so that we can hear your voice
amidst the busyness of intruding thoughts and dulled expectations,
so that we find ourselves impelled by joy
to announce your risen presence and life to our world.
We pray this in your name. Amen.

483. James the Apostle (25 July)

Challenge us, O Lord, by the example of your friend James;
his willingness to follow you as soon as you called him;
his support alongside you in the insecure days of being out on the roads,
facing welcome and danger, excitement and the unexpected;
and his ultimate faithfulness to the point
     of early martyrdom for your sake—
testimony that you do not measure commitment by length of service.
Challenge us, too, by your handling of his thunderous ways,
and by his ambitions for greatness in your kingdom
     at the expense of others.
Thank you that you never gave up on him;
and in your patient dealings with James
show us a template for your gracious work in us,
despite our mixed motives and confused ambitions.
May we be as faithful in our discipleship as he was.
In your holy name we pray. Amen.

484. The Blessed Virgin Mary as mother and disciple (15 August)

Remembering Mary's distress and fears
when Jesus was lost for three days
because his twelve-year-old priorities were different,
we pray for parents whose children's behaviour
    challenges them beyond their capacity to cope.
Remembering Mary's intervention
to ensure a great family wedding celebration,
we pray for families with events to celebrate
but who lack the resources to fulfil their dreams.
Remembering Mary's attempts to protect Jesus
    from exhaustion in ministry,
we pray for parents who watch their children burning out
and are torn between assisting them
and setting them free to carve their own way.
Remembering the widowed Mary's presence at the crucifixion,
we pray for parents who watch as their children suffer and die
and can offer nothing except their aching presence.
Remembering how Mary's presence was welcomed by the disciples
in the Upper Room while they prayed and waited
    for the empowering of the Holy Spirit,
we pray for women whose calling to serve you is dismissed
    or downplayed simply because they are women.
Gracious Lord, when you asked for Mary's "Yes" at the Annunciation,
your overshadowing gifted her for all she would face.
We pray today for women around the world
in need of such gifting today. Amen.

485. The Blessed Virgin Mary

We thank you, O heavenly Father, for feisty, vivacious women,
    who, having said "Yes" to an unimaginable vocation
get on faithfully with the lifetime of consequences.
As we celebrate the life of the Blessed Virgin Mary,
move us beyond the Annunciation to grasp her dependability
    throughout her son's life, death, resurrection and ascension.
Guide us to draw inspiration from her example,
and bless all women who, today, follow her footsteps
    of vibrant and faithful cooperation with your purposes.
We pray this in the name of Jesus Christ, her son, our Lord. Amen.

486. Bartholomew the Apostle (24 August)

For low-profile, utterly faithful Christians
who simply get on with whatever faces them
and never get their name in the headlines,
we praise you, O Lord.
For gracious people in whom there is no guile,
just utter fidelity to God and a transparent life with others,
we praise you, O Lord.
For people who are prepared to have their prejudices challenged
    and embrace the new and unexpected perspectives you lay before them,
then give their lives to following the consequences,
we praise you, O Lord.
For St Bartholomew, disciple, steady
companion and apostle to far nations,
we praise you, O Lord;
and we pray for the unfussy fidelity to follow his example. Amen.

487. Matthew, Apostle and Evangelist (21 September)

We pray for people who, like Matthew the tax collector,
gain wealth by exploiting others and are shunned and lonely.
We pray for the people they exploit who have no redress,
and for integrity in the financial institutions of the world.
We pray for people who, like Matthew,
find that you, Lord Jesus, are calling to them in their isolation
to follow you and turn their lives around.
We pray for people who feel there is no hope for them
to break free of destructive ways of life.
As you transformed Matthew's life, we pray
that you will suffuse their lives with hope and new life.
Show us how we play our part in bearing hope to this hurting world.
In your holy name we pray. Amen.

488. Matthew and his Gospel

As we remember Matthew and the three other Evangelists,
who took the time to collect and record the stories about Jesus,
we give thanks for the gift of their Gospels
with their different perspectives but common theme
of bearing witness to our Lord Jesus Christ.
Challenge us by Matthew's example
to pass on the good news that changed his life.
We pray for people who translate the scriptures
and for people who then read or hear them for the first time.
Open their ears to hear your gospel
that has brought life to people for two millennia,
and prosper its proclamation around the world today.
We pray this in the name of Jesus Christ our Lord,
to whom the Gospels bear glorious witness. Amen.

489. Michael and All Angels (29 September)

When we need strength, direction or protection,
keep us open, O Lord, to whatever way you come to us;
and, if you send an angel, then stop us from worrying what it looks like
and give us the gumption to hear your message through your messenger.
We pray in the name of Jesus Christ,
who knew the ministering of angels. Amen.

490. Luke the Evangelist (18 October)

Today when we remember Luke, Paul's beloved physician,
   who shared the dangers and delights of his travels,
tending his ongoing physical affliction
and patching him up when he was attacked,
we pray for all medical staff,
who use their training and skill in the service of others.
Give them wisdom in their research and diagnoses,
compassion in their caring
and stamina when they are exhausted from the demands placed on them.
We pray this in the name of Jesus Christ,
who himself healed the sick. Amen.

491. Luke and his Gospel

As we remember Luke and the three other Evangelists,
who took the time to collect and record the stories about Jesus,
we give thanks for the gift of their Gospels
with their different perspectives but common theme
 of bearing witness to our Lord Jesus Christ.
We thank you for Luke's orderly account of the good news
    in his Gospel and the Acts of the Apostles,
which recount the proclamation of salvation through Jesus Christ.
We pray for people who translate the Gospels,
so that the proclamation can continue in new languages,
and we pray for people who are reading or
    hearing the gospel for the first time.
We pray this in the name of Jesus Christ our Lord,
to whom the Gospels bear glorious witness. Amen.

492. Simon and Jude, Apostles (28 October)

Inspire us, Lord Jesus, with the passion and fervour
    of your apostles Simon and Jude,
who turned their zeal for potentially violent action
to secure political change into fervour to proclaim and give their lives
    for the gospel of the kingdom of God.
May we never condone the oppression of other people
but, like Simon and Jude, see beyond a response of aggression
to a response of commitment to the gospel
that brings release to the captives and liberty to the oppressed.
Give us courage to be tireless in our opposition to all that
    stunts the life and health of all people in your world.
We pray this in your name and for the welfare of your world. Amen.

493. St Jude as patron saint of lost causes

O God, when we feel that our life is hopeless and there is no one to help,

turn us, with St Jude, to trust in you

and grant us the joy of seeing mourning turn to dancing

when yet another hopeless cause bites the dust

and is transformed into a hope-filled new beginning.

We pray for people who have lost hope

    or never known what it is to hope.

In their loneliness and despair break through with new hope and joy.

We pray in the name of Jesus Christ,

who called Jude to be his disciple

and made of him an apostle to the nations. Amen.

494. Andrew the Apostle (30 November)

Thank you, O Lord, for Andrew's passion to bring other people to you:

his brother, Peter, who became a great apostle

the Greeks wanting to meet you,

whose arrival foreshadowed your Passion,

the boy with a picnic lunch which was seemingly inadequate,

but in your hands allowed 5,000 people to be fed.

Give us, like Andrew, the trust that if connections can be made

you will work miracles with what we offer.

In your name we pray. Amen.

495. Churches dedicated to St Andrew

We give you thanks, O Lord, for Andrew,
who left his fishing nets in Galilee to follow you,
never guessing that impulsive act would send him as far as
    Kiev and Novgorod as a messenger of the gospel.
We pray today for the churches around the world
which honour his part in their foundation
and look to Andrew as their patron saint.
May we dare to be as faithful in our time as he was in his,
even though he never lived to see the fruit of his brave labours.
We pray this in the name of Jesus Christ our Lord,
who first sent Andrew to fish for people. Amen.

496. Stephen, Deacon and First Martyr (26 December)

Yesterday, O God, we sang of peace on earth, goodwill to all people,
and today we remember the martyrdom of your servant, Stephen.
Forgive us, when we struggle
to keep these two stories of life and death together,
and help us to grasp the radical challenge of the Incarnation
    for the world into which your Son was born.
As we hear again the story of Stephen's death
and his peaceful entrusting of his life into your hands,
we pray for Christians who this Christmas
    have celebrated the Incarnation
in the face of persecution and the possibility of death
because of their faith in our Lord Jesus Christ.
May the peace of which the angels sang
permeate the places of fear and hatred in our world today.
We pray this in the name of the Prince of Peace,
our Saviour Jesus Christ. Amen.

497. John, Apostle and Evangelist (27 December)

Lord Jesus Christ,
today we honour your disciple John
for his witness to the Word made flesh who dwelt among us,
for his close friendship during your life,
for his trustworthiness in accepting the care of your mother,
for his faithfulness, despite his brother's early martyrdom,
for his steadfastness under persecution and long years of imprisonment,
for his training of Polycarp, who passed on his teaching and writings
and for the blend of his fiery personality with sublime experiences,
which are expressed in the Gospel and letters that bear his name.
As we remember and honour him,
teach us through his insights and example
to be as friendly and faithful in our day as he was in his.
In your holy name, we pray. Amen.

498. John, caring for other people's families

We remember, Lord Jesus, that you entrusted your elderly mother
    to the care of John, your friend and disciple.
We pray for people who care for other people's families
and for all who need that particular care:
people who are sick or aged,
people with severe disabilities or people with special needs.
We give thanks for nurses and care workers
and for people who over this Christmas season
are cleaning, maintaining or supplying care homes and hospitals.
Give them loving compassion in their contact with those they care for,
patience when care is rejected and delight in shared achievements.
Bless, too, all people who care for relatives within their own homes.
And while Christmas has brought no relief from the daily round of care
may it still be for them a season of joy and peace. Amen.

499. John and his Gospel

We give thanks, Lord Jesus Christ, for John
    and the three other Evangelists,
who took the time to collect and record the stories about Jesus,
and for the gift of their writings to the Church through the ages.
As we give thanks for John's Gospel and his letters,
with their testimony of having shared your life for three years
and heard, seen, looked at and touched you with his hands,
we pray that your light and love, to which he bore witness,
    will continue to shine out in the darkness of our world.
We pray this in your name, Lord Jesus Christ,
whom John knew and loved so steadfastly. Amen.

500. Holy Innocents (28 December)

As we remember the horror of the massacre
    of young boys in Bethlehem,
we pray for children whose lives are at risk today,
be it from tyrants like Herod,
the neglect or cruelty of those responsible for their care,
or the untended needs of food, shelter and medicine
that are the product of poverty, conflict or natural disaster.
Heavenly Father, you notice when a single sparrow falls to the ground;
protect the innocents who suffer today,
and challenge us all about our inadequate response to their needs.
We pray this in the name of Jesus Christ our Lord,
whose vulnerability as a baby we remember this Christmas season.
Amen.

Index: numerical

The needs of the world

General world needs

1   Inexpressible need

2   Response to suffering

3   Extreme horrors

4   Good citizenship

5   Building a righteous world

6   People in today's news

7   The victims of tragedy or terror

People with power or influence in the world

8   International relations

9   International relations

10   The United Nations and international organizations

11   The United Nations

12   World leaders

13   World leaders

14   World leaders

15   World leaders

16   World leaders and armed forces at times of tension

17   International or national crises

18   Integrity in public life

19   Sound advice and just action

20   Integrity in the media and communications

Justice and wellbeing for all

21   Justice

22   Acting for justice

23   Justice

24   Peace and justice for all

25   People living with injustice

26   Powerlessness

27   World inequality

28   Valuing difference

29   Fairness in international trade

War and peace

30   Broken dreams

31   An end to war

32   The victims of war

33   Long-standing enmity

34   War crimes

35   Terrorism and horrendous evil

36   Being peacemakers

37   Peaceful life in cities

38   Peace

Refugees and people in danger

39   Refugees

40   Refugees

41   Refugees

42   Children separated from their families

43   People who suffer

44   People in danger

45   People who have lost hope of relief

46   Forgotten news headlines

47   People who have lost their freedom

48   The aftermath of oppression

49   People who are oppressed

50   People who lack the essentials of life

51   Walking

52   Suffering that is no longer in the news

53   Rain

54   Water supplies

Disasters

55   Our response to disaster
56   People affected by natural disaster
57   Disaster
58   Pandemic
59   Epidemic or pandemic
60   Major accident
61   Forest fires

Rescue, emergency and aid workers

62   Relief workers
63   People who risk their lives for others

National and local life

Government and public life

64   Parliament
65   Administration of government
66   Integrity in public life
67   Financial constraint
68   Dissimulation in public life / Elections
69   The Royal Family and the armed services

National and local services

70   Unhealthy living environments
71   Children in cities
72   Riots
73   Damaged lives and unequal distribution of resources
74   Crime
75   Crime

76 Prisoners being released
77 Crime in the news
78 Murder
79 Homes that are dangerous
80 Places of safety
81 Trauma in life
82 Addictions
83 Addictions
84 Social Security and benefits
85 The misuse of resources
86 The emergency services
87 Undervalued workers
88 Immigration policy
89 Industrial relations
90 Farmers
91 The media
92 Facing adversity
93 Our shared citizenship
94 Difficult decisions in society
95 Needs and wants
96 Praying with the news

Local community life
97 Community life
98 Community life
99 Accessibility issues
100 Youth and community leaders
101 Road safety
102 Street life
103 Unsung people

Daily Life

Living faithfully

104   Faithful pilgrims

105   Faithful living

106   Ordinary living

107   Undramatic living

108   Ordinary time

109   Contentment

110   Following God in daily life

111   Exploring in life

112   Silence

113   Living with God's silence

114   Sitting down

115   Seeing life with God's eyes

116   Transformed living

117   The duties of life

118   In times of fear

119   God's presence in our lives

120   The gifts and demands of life

121   Focus in our busyness

122   When life is confusing

123   Contradictions and uncertainties in life

124   Unfamiliar territory

125   Wilderness living

126   Desert dryness

127   Reflecting God's glory

128   The goodness of God's love

129   Memories

130   Memories

131   Remembering past difficulties

132   Living well

133   Difficult decisions

134 Sharing our gifts
135 Overconfidence
136 Tensions
137 Joy in life
138 Joyful service
139 Enjoying God's presence
140 Enjoying God's world
141 God's love and light
142 Good news
143 Humour
144 Humour
145 Laughter
146 Being faithful when we are tempted to give up
147 Service in the face of need
148 Serving God in the world
149 Light in the world
150 Light in the world
151 Learning to love
152 Life as service
153 Responding to need
154 Prayer—not knowing how to pray
155 The history around us
156 Hurting each other
157 Holidays

Morning, noon and evening
158 Morning
159 Morning—stewardship of creation
160 Morning
161 Morning—Christ, whose glory fills the skies
162 Morning
163 Morning
164 Morning
165 Morning—for those facing difficulties

166   Morning
167   Midday
168   Midday—people in their work
169   Midday—suffering in the world
170   Evening
171   Evening—unfinished work
172   Evening—people who have suffered
173   Evening—people who work through the night
174   Evening—people who work through the night
175   Evening—sleep
176   Evening—sleep
177   Evening—rest
178   Evening—end of a busy day

Homes and hospitality
179   Hospitality
180   Welcoming homes
181   Hospitality and new beginnings

Work
182   Our daily work
183   Many kinds of work
184   People who clean up
185   Hard or demeaning work
186   Work at sea
187   Work in bad weather
188   Unemployment

Education and learning
189   Study
190   Study
191   Places of study
192   New academic term
193   Struggling at school

194   Struggling to learn

195   Exams

Creativity and the arts

196   Creativity

197   Music and / or art

198   Music

199   Creativity

200   Art therapy

201   Storytelling

Families and friends

Relationships

202   Family and friends

203   Family and friends

204   Family and friends

205   Friendship

206   Friendship

207   Friendship

208   Joy and refreshment

209   Family and community centres

210   People who are distant from us

211   Mothering / Mothering Sunday

212   Remembering the dead

People and families under stress or with special needs

213   Financial pressures

214   Families with special needs

215   Widowed people

216   Marriages under pressure
217   Broken families
218   Parents under pressure
219   Missing people
220   Strained relationships

Children
221   Children
222   Children's development
223   Children who are unsafe
224   Children with special needs
225   Children's delight
226   Adoption and fostering

Older people
227   Older people
228   God's faithfulness through life
229   Older people who need care
230   The restrictions of old age
231   Older Christians
232   Age and infirmity
233   Grandparents
234   Older people and children

People in need

People in need
235   People who are hurting
236   Isolated people
237   Loneliness, our response

238 Separation
239 Restricted lives
240 Intense suffering
241 Intense suffering
242 The harshness of life
243 People who seek for God
244 Looking for hope
245 Unnoticed suffering
246 Lack of freedom
247 Families under pressure
248 Children who are unsafe
249 Young people at risk
250 Parents whose dreams for their children are shattered
251 Unmet needs
252 Needs we ignore
253 Neglected compassion
254 Sensitivity to need
255 Fragile lives
256 Sources of hope and help
257 Wilderness and storm
258 All kinds of need
259 Unspoken prayers

People in poverty
260 Poverty
261 People with inadequate housing
262 Hunger
263 Foodbanks
264 Debt

People who are overwhelmed, in despair or grieving
265 Lost hope after disaster
266 Hope and healing
267 Confusion and distress

268   Grief

269   People who grieve

270   People needing solace

271   People who yearn for hope

272   Despair

273   Tears

274   Grief and confusion

275   People who grieve without hope

276   The loneliness and disorientation of grief

277   The death of a baby

278   People who grieve

279   Living with the fear of death

280   Regret

281   Destroyed dreams

282   Facing emergencies and life's nightmares

283   Earthquakes in life

284   The storms of life

285   The storms of life

286   Tragedy

Sickness and suffering

287   Healing

288   Healing

289   Pain

290   Women in labour

291   Children who are sick

292   Mental health concerns

293   Mental health concerns

294   People who are confused

295   Dementia

296   Memories

297   Long illness

298   Incurable disease

299   Terminal illness or living with unmeetable needs

300   Long-term illness
301   Long-term treatment
302   The impact of sickness

People who respond to need
303   Compassionate people
304   Nurses
305   Medical research
306   Hospices
307   Watching with those who are dying
308   The caring professions
309   Carers
310   Carers and medical staff
311   People who care
312   Caring for others
313   Respect for others
314   Action for those who suffer
315   Commitment to people in need
316   Volunteers who make a difference
317   People who make a difference

Creation

The wonder of creation
318   The wonder of creation
319   Creation's praise
320   The wonder of the world
321   The world's unexpected delights
322   The wonder of the world
323   The beauty of the seasons

324   Beauty and creativity
325   The changing seasons
326   Weather
327   Gardens
328   Sunsets
329   The night sky and space research
330   The Book of Nature
331   Spring
332   Autumn
333   Animals
334   Walking in the countryside

Stewardship of the world

335   The world as gift
336   Wise stewardship
337   Protecting creation
338   Stewardship of God's world
339   Exploring and caring for creation
340   The joy and despoliation of nature

Litanies

341   Litany for daily life
342   Long litany
343   Litany for the world
344   Litany for creation

The Church

The local church

345   The local church

346   The local church

347   Cathedrals and churches

348   Historic cathedrals and churches

349   Church buildings

350   Silence and church buildings

351   The ministry of the local church

352   The church community

353   Unity in the community

354   Our common life

355   Community

356   Saying goodbye to community members

357   Service

358   Responding faithfully

359   Sunday Schools and youth groups

360   The scriptures

Vocations in the Church

361   Vocations

362   Church leaders

363   Church leaders

364   New ministry

365   Leadership in the local church

366   Deacons

367   Priests

368   Bishops

369   Monastic life

370   Team ministry

371   Pastoral ministry

372   Using our particular gifts

Discipleship and mission

373   The call of Jesus

374   Following Jesus

375   God's call

376   Vocation and commitment

377   Saying "Yes" to God

378   The call of God

379   Vocation and pilgrimage

380   God's coming to us

381   Daring mission

382   Commitment to service

383   Commitment to discipleship

384   Following Jesus

385   Walking with God

386   Walking with Jesus

387   Life's pilgrimage

388   Living faithfully

389   Benedictine living

390   Stability in life

391   Formation by God—lessons from stonemasons

392   The song of angels in our lives

393   Contemplation

394   Retreats and retreat houses

395   Spiritual directors and guides

396   New ways to serve God in the world

397   Mission in the local community

398   Missionaries

399   People finding their way to faith

400   God's dynamic life

401   Christian unity

Baptism, marriage and funerals

402   The birth or baptism of a child

403   Baptism of an adult or child

404   Baptism of a baby or child

405   Marriage

406   Recent or future marriage

407   Renewal of marriage vows

408   Bereavement

409   Bereavement (including difficult memories)

410   People who mourn

411   People who mourn

Saints and Seasons

412   The Church year

Advent

413   Advent litany

414   Disturbance and hope

415   Wake up

416   Advent expectation

417   Advent amidst the winter scenery

418   Openness to God

419   People in need as Christmas approaches

Christmas

420   Open to God

421   Nativity petitions

422   Peace on earth

423   The Naming and Circumcision of Jesus

424   New Year

Epiphany

425   Epiphany: revelation of Jesus Christ

426   Epiphany: holy curiosity

427   Epiphany: light shining in the darkness

428   Epiphany: perseverance

429   The Baptism of Christ

430   The Presentation of Christ in the Temple (Candlemas)

Lent and Passiontide

431   Ash Wednesday

432   The gift of Lent

433   Lent: resisting temptation

434   Lent: learning obedience

435   The grace of Lent

436   Walking faithfully in Lent

437   Steadfastness in Passiontide

438   Passiontide: suffering for the gospel

439   Palm Sunday

440   Holy Week

441   Maundy Thursday

442   Good Friday: the cross

443   Good Friday: the cries of the world

444   Good Friday: the peace of Jerusalem

Easter

445   Easter rejoicing

446   Easter: the empty tomb

447   Easter: grief and joy

448   Easter: Jesus the gardener

449   Easter: Jesus and Peter

450   The unexpectedness of resurrection

451   The Emmaus Road

452   Ascension Day

453   Ascension and wounds

Pentecost

454   Pentecost: the coming of the Holy Spirit

455   Pentecost: the Spirit of transformation

Other festivals

456   The Annunciation of our Lord to the Blessed Virgin Mary

457   The Annunciation in lives today

458   Annunciation: God's intervention in our lives

459   The Transfiguration of our Lord

460   Holy Cross Day

461   All Saints' Day

Saints' Days

462   The variety of saints

463   Saints

464   Our forebears in the faith

465   The Week of Prayer for Christian Unity

466   The Conversion of Paul

467   Joseph of Nazareth

468   George, Martyr

469   Mark the Evangelist

470   Mark and his Gospel

471   Philip and James, Apostles

472   Matthias the Apostle

473   The Visit of the Blessed Virgin Mary to Elizabeth

474   Barnabas the Apostle

475   The Birth of John the Baptist

476   Peter and Paul, Apostles

477   Peter and Paul: commitment

478   Peter and Paul: people who differ

479   Thomas the Apostle

480   Mary Magdalene

481   Mary Magdalene: the example of her response

482   Mary Magdalene: being called by name

483   James the Apostle
484   The Blessed Virgin Mary as mother and disciple
485   The Blessed Virgin Mary
486   Bartholomew the Apostle
487   Matthew, Apostle and Evangelist
488   Matthew and his Gospel
489   Michael and All Angels
490   Luke the Evangelist
491   Luke and his Gospel
492   Simon and Jude, Apostles
493   St Jude as patron saint of lost causes
494   Andrew the Apostle
495   Churches dedicated to St Andrew
496   Stephen, Deacon and First Martyr
497   John, Apostle and Evangelist
498   John, caring for other people's families
499   John and his Gospel
500   The Holy Innocents

Index: alphabetical

abuse 22, 42, 43, 49, 202

accidents 60

addiction 44, 47, 71, 80, 82, 83, 218,
    247, 249

adoption and fostering 222, 223,
    224, 226, 467

Advent 413, 414, 415, 416, 417, 418,
    419

agriculture 90

Amnesty International 25

animals 183, 333

Annunciation 456, 457, 458

armed forces 16, 17, 36, 69, 186

arts and creativity 134, 183, 196,
    197, 198, 199, 200, 201, 324

Ascension Day 452, 453

Ash Wednesday 431

baptism 402, 403, 404, 429
    of Christ 429

bereavement 202, 275, 277, 408,
    409, 410, 411, 419, *see also death
    and dying*

Bible translation, *see Scripture*

Busyness 114, 121, 482

calling 361, 373, 374, 375, 378, 379,
    380, 465

Candlemas 430

carers and caring organizations 92,
    173, 223, 288, 295, 300, 302, 307,
    308, 309, 310, 311, 312, 317, 498

Children 70, 71, 193, 221, 222, 223,
    224, 225, 226, 234, 404

at risk 39, 40, 41, 42, 44, 47, 218,
    221, 223, 238, 248, 249, 500

child soldiers 42, 47

death 277

orphans 221

sick 291

special needs 193, 194, 214, 224

Christmas 392, 412, 419, 420, 421,
    422, 423

Church 345, 346, 347, 348, 350, 455

buildings 345, 347, 348, 349, 350,
    391

community 352, 353, 354, 355,
    356

leaders 362, 363, 364, 365, 367,
    368, 370

local 345, 346, 370, 397

mission and ministry 351, 352,
    357, 365, 372, 381, 396, 397,
    398, 451, 452, 481, 494, 495

monastic life 173, 369, 389

new ministry 364

ordained and licensed lay
    ministers 366, 367, 368, 370

pastoral and healing
    ministry 256, 266, 288, 371

persecuted 438, 468, 496

renewal 455

service 357

Sunday School and youth
    groups 359

unity 353, 401, 465

Church year 412,
    see also the separate seasons

cities 37, 70, 71, 72, 99, 444

citizenship 4, 5, 93

commitment 104, 108, 376, 377, 378, 379, 380, 382, 383, 400, 449, 456, 466, 471, 472, 477, 479, 481, 483, 485

Commonwealth 69

community life 71, 97, 98, 99, 100, 103, 209

 neighbourliness 308, 316, 317

compassion 152, 239, 253, 255, 270, 303, 397, 481

confusion, *see dementia*

contemplation 393

contentment 109

corruption 47

courts 74, 78

cousins 475

Creation 344

 beauty and wonder 109, 140, 318, 319, 320, 321, 322, 323, 324, 326, 327, 328, 329, 331, 334, 344, 394

 despoliation 336, 337, 338, 339, 340

 seasons 322, 323, 325, 330, 331, 332, 417

 stewardship 4, 58, 61, 85, 90, 159, 318, 319, 323, 327, 329, 335, 336, 337, 338, 339, 340, 344

creativity 134, 196, 199, 324

crime and its victims 71, 74, 75, 76, 77, 78, 82, 247

crisis and adversity 17, 92, 122, 123, 257, 267, 281, 282, 283, 284, 285

cross 442, 460

cruelty 34, 35, 48, 235, 413

curiosity 426

danger 40, 42, 44, 51

dangerous or adverse situations 44, 51, 118, 260

death, dying and bereavement 212, 215, 275, 277, 279, 307, 408, 409, 410, 411, *see also grief*

debt 213, 264

decisions 133

dementia 229, 294, 295

despair 265, 267, 270, 272, 280, 293

difference 28, 478

 physical challenges and special needs 39, 99, 215, 246

disasters 43, 52, 55, 56, 57, 58, 59, 60, 61

 natural disasters 43, 53, 54, 56, 61

discipleship 104, 110, 111, 315, 373, 381, 383, 384, 385, 386, 387, 391, 392, 400, 449, 459, 469, 471, 474, *see also calling*

discrimination 22

doctors, *see medical workers*

domestic violence 43, 44, 73, 79, 80, 202, 218

doubts 122, 131, 274, 434, 446

drought 326

drugs, *see addictions*

duties and responsibilities 117, 120, 146, 178

Easter 445, 446, 447, 448, 449, 450, 451

education and learning 189, 190, 191, 192, 193, 194, 195

elections 68

emergencies 55, 282

emergency services 35, 46, 55, 56, 57, 60, 61, 62, 63, 77, 80, 86, 168, 173, 288, 308, *see also relief workers*

encountering God 113, 115, 116, 118, 119, 127

encouragement 474

enemies 33, 35

Epiphany 425, 426, 427, 428, 429, 430

evening 170, 171, 172, 173, 174, 175, 176, 177, 178

evil 32, 35, 47

exams 195

family and friends 202, 203, 204, 209, 210, 475

   birth of a baby 290, 402, 473, 475

   care 309, 498

   domestic violence 43, 44, 73, 79, 80, 202, 218

   foster parents, *see adoption and fostering*

   parenting and grandparenting 40, 211, 218, 222, 223, 233, 250, 467, 484

   people without support 209

pressures in family life 202, 213, 214, 215, 216, 217, 218, 219, 220, 247, 250, 260, 300, 302

separation in families 39, 41, 42, 238

sickness within 291, 292, 295, 298, 302

special needs 214, 224, 229

trauma 60, 78

widows 215

famine 48, 50

farmers 90, 183

fear 118, 122, 246, 279

finance 67, 168, 213, 264, 481, 487

finding faith 399

fire 61

floods 53, 54, 326

food 90, 181, 262, 263

foodbanks 260, 263, 308

freedom / loss of freedom 47, 48, 49, 246

friendship 204, 205, 206, 207, 208, 209, 210, 497

gangs 47, 71, 74, 80

gardens 327

generosity 474

gifts and skills 134

God's glory and love 127, 128, 141, 425

Good Friday 442, 443, 444

Government 18, 19, 64, 65, 66, 67, 68

grief 212, 215, 239, 268, 269, 270, 273, 274, 275, 276, 277, 278, 286, 447

guidance 489

harvest 90

hatred and hate crimes 22, 34, 43, 44, 247

healing 45, 200, 266, 287, 288, 291, 304

helpers 103

history 155

holidays 157

Holy Cross Day 460

Holy Spirit 454, 455, 474

Holy Week 412

homelessness 43, 44, 45, 50, 176, 261

homes 180
  unsafe or unhealthy 70, 79, 80, 176, 261

hope 244, 413, 414, 487
  amidst difficulty 33, 45, 241, 244, 256, 265, 266, 271, 272, 275, 285, 286, 414, 487, 493
  loss of hope 45

hospices and hospitals 46, 77, 288, 306

hospitality 179, 180, 181

housing management 261

human trafficking and modern slavery 42, 47, 80

humour 143, 144, 145

hunger 241, 262, 263

immigration 88, 94

industry and industrial relations 89, 183

inequality 27

injustice 21, 22, 25, 26

international relations 8, 9, 10, 11, 16, 17, 29, 33, 99

Jerusalem (peace) 37, 444

joy and delight 109, 128, 137, 138, 139, 140, 141, 142, 143, 208, 225, 420, 445, 447, 482

judgement 415

justice 21, 22, 23, 24, 30, 78, 441

laughter 143, 144, 145, 180

Lent 431, 432, 433, 434, 435, 436

life
  busyness 114, 121, 482
  daily life 105, 106, 107, 108, 109, 110, 111, 114, 132, 341, 418
  difficulties and disappointments 118, 122, 123, 124, 125, 126, 133, 194, 280, 281, 282, 283, 284, 285, 286
  duties and responsibilities 117, 120, 146, 178
  encountering God 113, 115, 116, 118, 119, 127
  faithful living 104, 105, 132, 134, 135, 150, 151, 358, 377, 385, 386, 387, 388, 389, 390, 392, 400, 471, 472, 486
  harshness 241, 242
  joy 128, 137, 138, 139, 140, 142, 143, 145

light in darkness 149, 150, 427, 444, 499

Litanies 341, 342, 343, 344, 413

loneliness 209, 215, 236, 237, 238, 276, 293

marriage 216, 405, 406, 407

Maundy Thursday 441

media 20, 91

medical workers 46, 59, 168, 173, 288, 289, 297, 298, 304, 305, 310, 490

memories 33, 45, 129, 130, 131, 296, 409, 419

mental health 246, 292, 293

midday 167, 168, 169

missing people 217, 219, 247

mission and ministry 351, 352, 357, 365, 372, 381, 396, 397, 398, 451, 452, 481, 494, 495

missionaries 398

monastic life 173, 369, 389

money, *see finance*

morning 158, 159, 160, 161, 162, 163, 164, 165, 166

mourning, *see death*

murder 78

music 197, 198

Naming and Circumcision of Jesus 423

natural disaster 43, 53, 54, 56, 61, 498

natural resources 85

need, people in 6, 7, 32, 45, 47, 50, 94, 95, 96, 235, 236, 237, 258, 259, 265, 266, 267, 270, 281, 282, 282, 419

continuing need 46, 48, 52

danger 40, 42, 44, 51

inexpressible or overwhelming need 1, 35, 46, 56, 147

our response 2, 3, 4, 5, 43, 55, 92, 96, 110, 138, 147, 153, 154, 252, 254, 255, 262

sources of help 256, 280

unmet need 251, 252, 253, 256

new beginnings 181, 487

New Year 424

news 6, 7, 46, 91, 96

National Health Service (NHS) 94, 304

nurses, *see medical workers*

obedience 377, 434

older people 39, 40, 209, 216, 227, 228, 229, 230, 231, 232, 233, 234

online bullying 20

openness to God 128, 135, 139, 140, 189, 257, 392, 400, 418, 420, 489

oppression 15, 47, 48, 49, 73, 414, 481, 492

orphans 221

pain 176, 289, 302

Palm Sunday 439

pandemic 58, 59

Passiontide and Holy Week 437, 438, 439, 440, 441, 442, 443, 444

peace and peacemaking 24, 30, 33, 36, 38, 422, 444, 496

Pentecost 454, 455

people at risk 47, 70

perseverance 146, 428

pets 333

pilgrimage 104, 379, 387

police 71, 74, 77, 78, 79, 86, 308, *see also emergency services*
politicians 64, 67, 80, 92, 168
pollution 50, 70
poverty 43, 213, 218, 260, 261, 262, 263, 264
power 17, 18
powerlessness 26
prayer 154, 258, 259
pregnancy and birth of a baby 290, 402, 473, 475
Presentation of Christ 430
prisons and prisoners 74, 75, 76, 78, 238, 261
    political prisoners 47
probation services 71, 74, 76
public life and government 18, 19, 64, 65, 66, 67, 68, 173

race relations 28, 44, 93
rain 53
reconciliation 31, 33, 136
refugees 39, 40, 41, 44, 45, 51, 94, 238
refuges and places of safety 80, 223
regret 280
relationships 28, 136, 313
    hurt 156, 216
    relief and emergency workers 35, 46, 55, 56, 57, 62, 63
    unhealthy or dangerous 73, 220
rescue 46
research 59, 183, 298, 305, 329, 339

resources
    distribution 67, 73, 80, 84, 85, 94
    misuse 85
respect for others 313
response to suffering and need 2, 3, 4, 5, 36, 43, 55, 92, 96, 110, 138, 147, 149, 153, 251, 252, 254, 255, 262, 286, 303, 307, 312, 313, 314, 315
restoration 46
restrictions in life 239, 246
retreats 394
riots 72
road and transport safety 101
Royal Family 69

sadness and sorrow 45, 239, 259
safety and places of safety 39, 40, 41, 45, 50, 74, 80, 101, 216, 219, 223, 248, 293, 342
saints 458, 459, 460, 461
    All Saints Day 461
    Andrew the Apostle 494, 495
    Barnabas the Apostle 474
    Bartholomew the Apostle 486
    Elizabeth 231, 473, 475
    George, Martyr 468
    Holy Innocents 500
    James the Apostle 483
    John the Baptist 475
    John, Apostle and Evangelist 497, 498, 499
    Joseph of Nazareth 467
    Luke the Evangelist 490, 491
    Mark the Evangelist 469, 470

Mary 418, 456, 457, 458, 473, 484, 485

Mary Magdalene 448, 480, 481, 482

Matthew, Apostle and Evangelist 47, 487, 488

Matthias the Apostle 472

Michael and All Angels 489

Paul 465, 466, 476, 477, 478

Peter 449, 476, 477, 478

Peter and Paul, Apostles 476, 477, 478

Philip and James, Apostles 471

Simon and Jude, Apostles 492, 493

Stephen, Deacon and First Martyr 496

Thomas the Apostle 446, 479

Visitation 473

saying goodbye 356

school and university 191, 192, 193, 194, 195

Scripture 360, 470, 488, 491, 499

sea and sailors 186

seeking God 243, 244

serving God 138, 147, 148, 149, 150, 151, 152, 357, 382, 384, 386, 396

sickness 289, 291, 419

    incurable or long-term 297, 298, 299, 300, 301, 302

    medical research 59, 298

silence, quiet and stillness 112, 113, 114, 350, 393, 394, 414

sleep and rest 175, 176, 177

social security 84

social services 71, 79, 168, 203, 217, 218, 223, 226, 249, 260, 288, 308

special needs 193, 194, 214, 224

spiritual directors 395

steadfastness 146, 376, 390, 436, 437

stewardship, see creation

study 189, 190

suffering 2, 3, 7, 43, 45, 48, 52, 56, 57, 169, 172, 235, 240, 241, 268, 419

    intense 3, 35, 240, 241, 286, 299

    our response 2, 36, 43, 55, 149, 251, 252, 253, 254, 255, 286, 303, 307, 312, 313, 314, 315

    prayer for God's presence 250, 272, 274, 275, 280, 281, 282, 283, 284, 285, 298, 299, see also grief

    unnoticed 52, 245, 253, 259

    world 414, 440, 443

sunsets 328

teachers 92, 168, 190, 192, 193, 317, see also education

tears 235, 239, 268, 269, 273

temptation 433

terrorism 7, 35

trade 29

tragedy 7, 60, 286

Transfiguration of our Lord 459

trauma 78, 81, 265, 266, 267, 281, 282, 283, 284, 285, 286

trust in God 257, 281, 284

unemployment 188, 202, 296

United Nations 10, 11

urban life 70, 71, 72, 99, 102

   riots 72

   street life 102

violence 42, 78, 79, 202, 247

vocation 361, 369, 372, 375, 376, 379, 396

volunteers 103, 263, 316

vulnerable people 26, 32, 43, 44, 45, 47, 48, 49, 50, 51, 80, 238, 246, 255

   children 42, 71

wake-up call 415, 416

walking 51, 334

war 24, 31, 33

   end to 31

   victims of 30, 32, 34, 35, 46

   war crimes 34

water supplies 50, 53, 54, 326

weather 53, 187, 326

work and workers 87, 97, 103, 158, 168, 171, 182, 183, 184, 185, 186, 187, 238

   demeaning 49, 188

   night workers 173, 174

   undervalued 87, 184, 185, 187

world 5, 343, 414, 440, 443

   international relations 8, 9, 10, 11, 16, 29

   leaders 9, 12, 13, 14, 15, 16, 17, 18, 19

   oppressive regimes 48

   world needs 1, 6, 17, 35, 44, 46, 48, 50, 52, 440

worries 358

youth and children's work 71, 100, 249, 359

youth and community 100, 249, 359

Lightning Source UK Ltd.
Milton Keynes UK
UKHW022049160223
417160UK00003B/460